31 Intentional Days Of Life Transformation

By Experiencing Quality Wisdom For A Modern Age

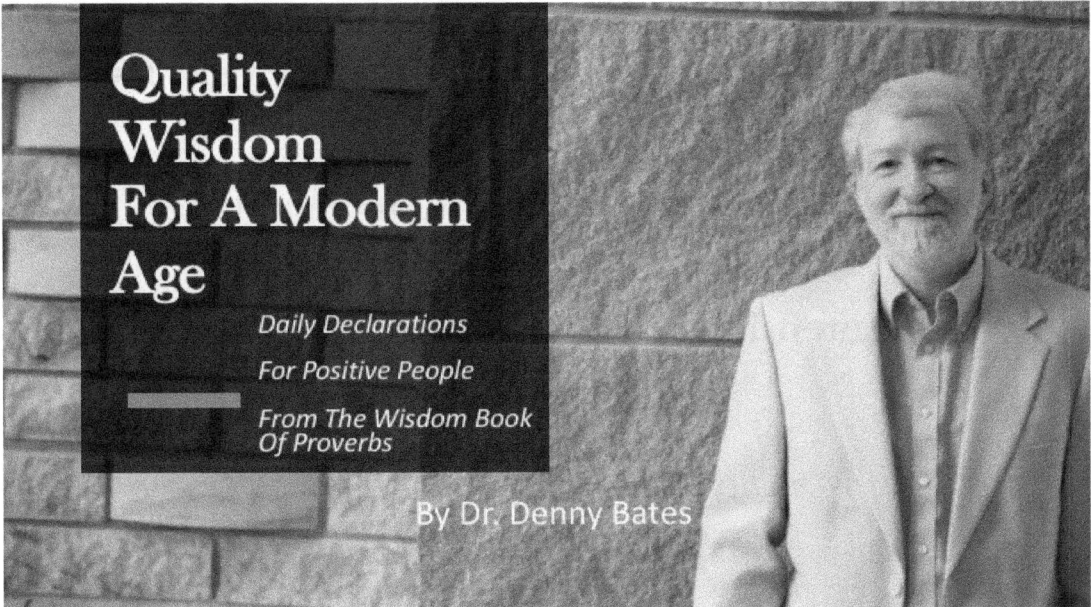

Quality
Wisdom
For A Modern
Age

Daily Declarations

For Positive People

From The Wisdom Book Of Proverbs

By Dr. Denny Bates

Become The Very Best Version Of You!

By

Making This Year Your Greatest Year Ever

When You Commit To The Process Of

31 Intentional Days Of Life Transformation

A Quality Leadership Personal Growth Course
by Dr. Denny Bates

31 Intentional Days Of Life Transformation:

Experiencing Quality Wisdom For A Modern Age

Daily Declarations For Positive People

Based On, Today May You In Proverbs:

The Quality Leader's Essential Guidebook For Personal, Professional, and Spiritual Growth

By Dr. Denny Bates

31 Intentional Days Of Life Transformation:

Experiencing Quality Wisdom For A Modern Age In Proverbs

Today May You In Proverbs

The Quality Leader's Essential Guidebook For

Personal, Professional, and Spiritual Growth

Something New Christian Publishers
E-Mail dennybates@gmail.com
On the Web: www.dennybates.com

You can "friend" me on Facebook at www.facebook.com/denny.bates
or follow me on Twitter @dennybates
www.TheQualityDisciple.com

Table Of Contents

31 Intentional Days Of Life Transformation

Dedication and Acknowledgements

There are the rare times in a life's journey where incredible people come across our path, stick. When we meet them for the first time, we might note their friendliness or how they made an impression and we figure, sooner or later, either we or "thee" will move on. I met Donald "DW" Worrell during my junior year at West Florence High School in 1972. In addition to taking classes together we were also in the same home room. He was a gifted athlete who had his dreams of fame and I was active in band, destined, in my own mind (at least), to be the eventual replacement for Doc Severinsen on The Tonight Show. But as the curious ups and downs of life became intrusive companions on each of our paths, both of us have been intentionally walking on the solid ground of our faith in Jesus. He has been our Rock on which we have stood for all of these years.

The way for us has not been an easy one. Both of us have suffered incalculable losses and both of us have experienced incredible joys, irresistible grace and lasting peace because of our trust in the One who does all things well. One of the first people I reached out to a few years ago when my personal life was in shambles was DW. Why? Because he's proven trustworthy and he listens, and he is wise and he's safe and he's my friend. He is also a man who has lived out his faith even when his own heart has been crushed by the loss of family and friends. DW is a man of CONSISTENCY, COURAGE, COMPASSION, and most of all, he is CHRIST-CENTERED. How do I know? Because I've seen him do it for over 40 years, and if you have known him for any length of time you have too.

As I thought about to whom I would dedicate this book, my answer became obvious. I want to dedicate *31 Intentional Days of Life Transformation* to a man who not only loves the Word of God but a man, who by grace, seeks to live out it's eternal life principles before us every day, showing all of us a clear example of a transformed life. This is for you DW: A brother and a devoted friend who keeps on pressing on!

Dr. Denny Bates

February 2020

Acknowledgements

My books are so much better because of those who willingly volunteer their time to read through the sample proof and make sure, first and foremost, that the contents speak to the heart first and then to the mind. They are also people of good grammar and watch out for those pesky typos that get by me, but not them. I am grateful to Bryan Braddock, Amy Watts, Reeves Cannon, Dick Brown, Tamara Rhodes, Lisa Ray, Traci McCombs, Amy Clark, Ron Lyles, Wick Jackson, Patty Smith, Leslie Rutten, Laura Harris, Cleo Corey, Carol Mabe, and Kirby King.

FOREWORD

There are a very select few people that you will find in life that are just as passionate about your success as you are. Usually your greatest support team will be your mother, father, spouse, grand-parent or a very close childhood friend. Seldom if ever do you come across someone later in life that sees something in you that you no longer see in yourself and will come along side of you as your biggest cheerleader. That miracle someone came in my life in the form of Denny Bates. At a time when my mother and greatest cheerleader had just passed away, my father-in-law had passed away and my wife, Tracey, and I were doing the best we could to prop each other up during our time of grief is when I met Dr. Denny Bates.

I remember vividly meeting our first time in person at Panera Bread for lunch. Because of some mutual friends we had become connected on Facebook, so we had a little knowledge of each other via the Facebook filtered lens. We all know that Facebook is a promotional tool for the best parts of our life and the life we want everyone to think we live. So, through this lens I knew Denny as the local encouraging Rockstar from Aisle 31 at the local hardware store. This guy had his picture taken with every local in town who was a celebrity in the city of Florence, SC. Preachers, local politicians, community movers and shakers as well as the longtime community legacies in our small city were displayed in hundreds of pictures with Dr. Denny Bates. I had to meet this guy and see if he was the real deal. It didn't take me long in our conversation to see his genuineness. He was transparent, humble, aware of his failures yet sure of his calling. That calling is to help and encourage others.

I sensed an immediate connection and brotherhood with Denny. I knew that we would be lifelong friends. He was what we all need in life. Someone that will listen to us, connect with us and passionately encourage us. There is no lack of people that will tell you what you can't do in life but few that will not only support what you think you can do while encouraging you that you can achieve far more.

Denny has helped me in many ways. We have enjoyed fellowship over a meal, been in Bible studies together and worked on projects together. He is great at one on one and that connection is what he brings to his book "Quality Wisdom for A Modern Age." You will get to know Dr. Denny Bates personally as he takes you through a spiritual growth process using the greatest book on wisdom ever written. Denny presents the biblical truths of the book of Proverbs to help you believe in you and he encourages you all along the way. Even non-believers use the principles of Proverbs in their self-help books, but they don't understand the true power of these principles and that is having a relationship with Jesus Christ.

Denny makes sure that he doesn't leave you believing that applying these principles may work for others. He makes sure you believe that they will work for you and encourages you every step of the way. I have been blessed to come to know Denny and call him my friend. I am certain that you will be blessed to get to know him through this book and that you too will find a lifelong friend in Dr. Denny Bates.

Proverbs 18:24 "A man that hath friends must shew himself friendly: and there is a friend that sticketh closer than a brother."

Bryan A. Braddock
Executive Director of the House of Hope

Forward Focused LLC
www.forwardfocusedllc.com

What Notable Theologians Say About the Book of Proverbs

Charles Spurgeon on The Book of Proverbs:

"The Proverbs appear at first sight to be thrown together without connection, but it is not so: when you come to close reading you will discover that they are threaded pearls, and that they are in proper position with regard to each other."

Billy Graham on the Book of Proverbs:

"The Psalms tell us how to get along with God, and the Proverbs tell us how to get along with our fellow man."

Nate Pickowicz on the Book of Proverbs:

"The beautiful thing about the wisdom of Proverbs is that it's timeless. While textbooks often need updating, Proverbs hasn't had a 2nd edition in three millennia!"

The Book of Proverbs *is* the pathway towards Growing in Greatness!

[5] Trust in the LORD with all your heart; do not depend on your own understanding.
[6] Seek his will in all you do, and he will show you which path to take.
Proverbs 3:5-6 (NLT)

"God does not give us everything we want, but He does fulfill His promises, leading us along the best and straightest paths to Himself." – **Dietrich Bonhoeffer**

This wonderful and timeless book of Proverbs will be the path that will, as Bonhoeffer says, lead us along the best and straightest paths to Himself.

QUALITY QUOTES FOR THE QUALITY LEADER WHO DESIRES TO GROW:

"Transformation is not five minutes from now; it's a present activity. In this moment you can make a different choice, and it's these small choices and successes that build up over time to help cultivate a healthy self-image and self-esteem." —JILLIAN MICHAELS

"Transformation literally means going beyond your form." —WAYNE DYER

"Transformation is a process, and as life happens there are tons of ups and downs.
It's a journey of discovery." —RICK WARREN

"Income seldom exceeds personal development." —JIM ROHN

"You cannot dream yourself into a character; you must hammer and forge yourself one."
—HENRY DAVID THOREAU

"Personal development is a major time-saver. The better you become, the less time it takes you to achieve your goals." —BRIAN TRACY

"The only person you are destined to become is the person you decide to be."
—RALPH WALDO EMERSON

"There is nothing noble in being superior to your fellow man; true nobility is being superior to your former self." —ERNEST HEMINGWAY

"When we are no longer able to change a situation, we are challenged to change ourselves."
—*Viktor E. Frankl*

"Of course motivation is not permanent. But then, neither is bathing; but it is something you should do on a regular basis." – *Zig Ziglar*

"As the physically weak man can make himself strong by careful and patient training, so the man of weak thoughts can make them strong by exercising himself in right thinking." – *James Allen*

"Growth is the great separator between those who succeed and those who do not. When I see a person beginning to separate themselves from the pack, it's almost always due to personal growth."
—JOHN C. MAXWELL

'And I am certain that God, who began the good work within you, will continue his work until it is finally finished on the day when Christ Jesus returns.' (Philippians 1:6 NLT) –*The Apostle Paul*

'But if you remain in me and my words remain in you, you may ask for anything you want, and it will be granted! When you produce much fruit, you are my true disciples. This brings great glory to my Father.' (John 15:7-8 NLT)—*Jesus*

Can you imagine what your life will look like this same time next year *IF*

you saw incredible growth . . .

> In your PERSONAL life
>
> In your PROFESSIONAL life
>
> In your SPIRITUAL life

Would you agree, for you, it would have been a very good year? I believe I can answer for you. YES!!!

Well, I have just what you need to turn an okay year into a great one.

31 Intentional Days Of Life Transformation
By Experiencing Quality Wisdom For A Modern Age In Proverbs

SPECIAL FEATURES OF
"31 Intentional Days Of Life Transformation"

"31 Days Of Life Transformation" Is A Book For . . .

❖ Busy People!	❖ Business Leaders	❖ Parents
❖ Students	❖ Pastors	❖ Teachers
❖ Small Group Leaders	❖ Civic Leaders	❖ Government Leaders
❖ Counselors	❖ Doctors	❖ Lawyers
❖ The New Christian	❖ The Seasoned Christian	❖ The Not Sure

❖ 31 full sessions, with thirty-one days of devotions and Bible studies in each session that are easy to read and practically apply to one's life in five minutes or less or for a deeper study, a self-taught practical Bible study is included.

❖ Positive declarations of prayer that will seal each devotional truth in one's heart.

❖ 31 daily devotions designed to move the reader to experience a transformational life change.

❖ 31 sessions that are designed to cause growth in one's personal, professional, and spiritual life.

❖ Each passage of Scripture written out, using the modern, easy to understand and read, New Living Translation (NLT).

❖ Formatted in a convenient workbook size that gives the reader plenty of space for taking notes.

❖ Strategically designed for use in small groups and as sermon prep and classroom studies.

❖ The perfect gift for the person who loves the Book of Proverbs.

Some Suggestions On How To Use 31 Intentional Days Of Life Transformation:

- You can use this spiritual growth resource as a daily devotion. It is designed as a tool you can use as a devotion and a Bible study: You can use it in the morning before you begin your day and at night, at the end of your day. *You can also customize this resource and turn it into a small group study!*

- Contained in each devotional entry is The Day, The Title of The Devotion, The Proverb, The Positive Confession of "Today May You," and then the POSITIVE DECLARATIONOF QUALITY WISDOM written as a Prayer Of Commitment.

- This spiritual growth resource is set up as a thirty-one-day exercise, it can be adapted to your lifestyle. In other words, use what you need and then set aside the rest for another time. Your goal is not speed. Your goal needs to be spiritual growth.

If you decide you want to take the daily approach, here is what you will experience:

- A passage of Scripture you can read and then let it set your spiritual framework for the rest of the day. Look for <u>key words</u> and <u>phrases</u> that you can mull over.

- For each daily Scripture there also is a "POSITIVE DECLARATIONOF QUALITY WISDOM" which is your declaration for the day. It may help you better grasp the power of what you are reading by reading it aloud several times at the beginning and throughout the day.

- You will be presented with a few concise points of commentary based upon the passage called *Quality Wisdom Devotional Thought* that will give you a better understanding.

- After you read the declaration you will be invited to personalize your declaration by offering it as a prayer. It might help you to also read this prayer aloud. Resist the temptation to rush through this spiritual experience. Words have meaning. Ponder each one of these precious words as you pray over each one.

- Each day also includes focused questions called **Keys To Experiencing Quality Wisdom For Life.** Each key is a great resource for your own personal reflection time or as a group study.

- To enjoy a deep Bible Study there are Bible study prompts that will guide you to a deeper learning experience by going through the process of OBSERVATION, INTERPRETATION, and APPLICATION of the Bible passage.

- Finally, you will be asked to gauge how each *POSITIVE DECLARATIONOF QUALITY WISDOM* CHALLENGES you in your PERSONAL, PROFESSIONAL, and in your SPIRITUAL life.

A Special Note For Small Group Leaders

31 Intentional Days Of Life Transformation is structured in a way where the book is about "process" and not for speed reading. That said, you can lead your group in a variety of ways that best suits the needs of your group.

- ❖ **Path One**: 31 days in a row—this would be intensive, but very rewarding. If you choose this option, try to lead your group during a month that has 31 days in it.
- ❖ **Path Two**: If you go through the study materials over six weeks you would need to average about four and a half lessons per week to complete the study.
- ❖ **Path Three**: If you go through the study materials over ten weeks you would need to average about three lessons per week to complete the study.
- ❖ **Path Four**: If you go through the study materials over thirteen weeks you would need to average about two lessons per week to complete the study.
- ❖ **Path Five**: Allow the Spirit and the needs of your group lead you and go at a pace that works for everyone with no timeline to hinder the process of growth.

Personal, Professional, and Spiritual Goals

Hockey great Wayne Gretzky once remarked, "You miss 100% of the shots you don't take." You will maximize your efforts as you experience *31 Intentional Days Of Life Transformation* once you identify your goals and then implement them. Before you begin this study, take some time and prayerfully think through some of your goals in your Personal, Professional, and Spiritual Life. Then, use them as a point of reference you can refer back to as you go through the study materials.

Keep this great promise in mind as you work through this important exercise:

'Now all glory to God, who is able, through his mighty power at work within us, to accomplish infinitely more than we might ask or think. 'Ephesians 3:20

PERSONAL GOALS

Goal	What Is The First Thing I Can Do To Reach My Goal	My Greatest Obstacle In Reaching My Goal

PROFESSIONAL GOALS

Goal	What Is The First Thing I Can Do To Reach My Goal	My Greatest Obstacle In Reaching My Goal

SPIRITUAL GOALS

Goal	What Is The First Thing I Can Do To Reach My Goal	My Greatest Obstacle In Reaching My Goal

Covenant For Experiencing Quality Wisdom Commitment Page

All of us benefit when we can submit our goals to trusted friends who will kelp keep us accountable. By already picking up this book, you are already showing the first steps towards your "personal surrender" of your way, to the Lord's way. Carefully read the covenant written out for you below:

By God's grace and by His power, I _____ make the pledge to make the contents of this book a priority in my life (Pick one):

_____ over the next 31 days

_____ over the next 6 weeks

_____ over the next 10 weeks

_____ over the next 13 weeks

_____ at a pace as the Lord leads you

I pledge prayerfully make a list of my goals in my personal, professional, and spiritual life and then trust the Lord to work out the circumstances in me and around me.

I pledge to prayerfully read through each daily exercise and "listen" to the Lord's voice as He speaks to my heart through His Word and trust Him to cause me to experience life transformation.

_____

Sign Your Name Here   Date   Covenant Accountability Partner

My Intentional Bible Study Check List

You can use this checklist to measure your progress. Remember, the goal is not speed, it's change. It's not a race but a process.

Bible Study Lesson	Date Completed

DAY ONE: "A Life Of Influence"

DAY TWO: "High Value Wisdom"

DAY THREE: "The Keys To A Wildly Successful Life"

DAY FOUR: "Get Wisdom While You Can"

DAY FIVE: "Look Up Living"

DAY SIX: "Embracing The Mentored Life"

DAY SEVEN: "The Prize-Driven Life"

DAY EIGHT: "Wisdom Matters"

DAY NINE: "Time Investment"

DAY TEN: "Business Issues"

DAY ELEVEN: "God's GPS For You"

DAY TWELVE: "Love What Matters"

DAY THIRTEEN: "Tongue Twisters"

DAY FOURTEEN: "Right On!"

DAY FIFTEEN: "Word Diplomat"

DAY SIXTEEN: "No Limit To Your Dreams"

DAY SEVENTEEN: "Heart Check"

DAY EIGHTEEN: "Wisdom Source"

DAY NINTEEN: "got Honesty?"

Bible Study Lesson   **Date Completed**

Okay! Let's begin your journey into living out the great promises of *31 Intentional Days Of Life Transformation*. Your next step towards transformational growth begins on the next page.

DAY ONE: "A Life Of Influence"

Today May You . . . have a heart that is open to wisdom, a mind that is willing to be disciplined, and have an unswerving commitment to do what is right, just, and fair.

These are the proverbs of Solomon, David's son, king of Israel.

Their purpose is to teach people wisdom and discipline,

to help them understand the insights of the wise.

Their purpose is to teach people to live disciplined and successful lives, to help them do what is right, just, and fair. (Proverbs 1:1-3 NLT).

Quality Wisdom Devotional Thought:

Are you "teachable?" One of the greatest blessings a person can say about themselves is that they have a teachable spirit. If we are teachable, then we are able to be taught . . .

- Wisdom
- Discipline
- How to have a successful life
- What to do: what is right, just, and fair

Turn your POSITIVE DECLARATION OF QUALITY WISDOM into this prayer of commitment:

Lord Jesus, *Today May I have a heart that is open to wisdom, a mind that is willing to be disciplined, and have an unswerving commitment to do what is right, just, and fair.*

Keys To Experiencing Quality Wisdom For Life

What do you think is the key to having a heart that is teachable?

Going Deeper In Bible Study

*I'll give you a few prompts in **bold type** to get you started. Then you can select one or two key words, phrases or doctrines in this passage of Scripture and follow the process by going through the three key elements of doing a meaningful Bible study (Observation, Interpretation, and Application):

These are the proverbs of Solomon, David's son, king of Israel.

Their purpose is to teach people wisdom and discipline,

to help them understand the insights of the wise.

Their purpose is to teach people to live disciplined and successful lives, to help them do what is right, just, and fair. (Proverbs 1:1-3 NLT).

OBSERVATION: WHAT IS THE AUTHOR SAYING? {*key words, phrases or doctrines*}

INTERPRETATION: WHAT DOES IT MEAN? *{If you are doing a word study you may want to use a concordance. If you are studying a doctrine (a Biblical principle), can you give it a name? i.e., "the doctrine of . . . "}*

APPLICATION: HOW DOES IT APPLY TO ME? *{This is a key part of your Bible study. Read and pray through the Proverb again and review your thoughts on your notes on Observation and Interpretation then write out a concise personal application.}*

POSITIVE DECLARATION OF QUALITY WISDOM

Today May You . . . have a heart that is open to wisdom, a mind that is willing to be disciplined, and have an unswerving commitment to do what is right, just, and fair.

These are the proverbs of Solomon, David's son, king of Israel.

Their purpose is to teach people wisdom and discipline,

to help them understand the insights of the wise.

Their purpose is to teach people to live disciplined and successful lives, to help them

do what is right, just, and fair. (Proverbs 1:1-3 NLT).

HOW THIS PROVERB CHALLENGES ME . . .

In my PERSONAL life

In my PROFESSIONAL life

In my SPIRITUAL life

DAY TWO: "High Value Wisdom"

Today May You . . . place a HIGH VALUE on the Lord's wisdom and the grace He gives for you to understand what to do with His wisdom.

My child, listen to what I say,

and treasure my commands.

Tune your ears to wisdom,

and concentrate on understanding.

Cry out for insight,

and ask for understanding.

Search for them as you would for silver;

seek them like hidden treasures.

Then you will understand what it means to fear the Lord,

and you will gain knowledge of God. (Proverbs 2:1-5 NLT).

Quality Wisdom Devotional Thought:

What we value the most is what we often treasure the most too. When we are motivated by treasure, we embrace our personal priorities. In this case, as we treasure the Lord's commands, we will experience two amazing benefits:

- We will understand what it means to fear (have an awesome reverence for) the Lord
- We will gain in knowledge of God

Turn your POSITIVE DECLARATION OF QUALITY WISDOM into this prayer of commitment:

Lord Jesus, *Today May I place a HIGH VALUE on the Lord's wisdom and the grace He gives for me to understand what to do with His wisdom.*

Keys To Experiencing Quality Wisdom For Life

What do you think is the key to knowing what the difference is between treasure and trash?

Going Deeper In Bible Study

*I'll give you a few prompts in **bold type** to get you started. Then you can select one or two key words, phrases or doctrines in this passage of Scripture and follow the process by going through the three key elements of doing a meaningful Bible study (Observation, Interpretation, and Application):

My child, listen to what I say,

and treasure my commands.

Tune your ears to wisdom,

and concentrate on understanding.

Cry out for insight,

and ask for understanding.

Search for them as you would for silver;

seek them like hidden treasures.

Then you will understand what it means to fear the Lord,

and you will gain knowledge of God. (Proverbs 2:1-5 NLT).

OBSERVATION: WHAT IS THE AUTHOR SAYING? {*key words, phrases or doctrines*}

INTERPRETATION: WHAT DOES IT MEAN? *{If you are doing a word study you may want to use a concordance. If you are studying a doctrine (a Biblical principle), can you give it a name? i.e., "the doctrine of . . . "}*

APPLICATION: HOW DOES IT APPLY TO ME? *{This is a key part of your Bible study. Read and pray through the Proverb again and review your thoughts on your notes on Observation and Interpretation then write out a concise personal application.}*

POSITIVE DECLARATION OF QUALITY WISDOM

Today May You . . . place a HIGH VALUE on the Lord's wisdom and the grace He gives for you to understand what to do with His wisdom.

My child, listen to what I say,

and treasure my commands.

Tune your ears to wisdom,

and concentrate on understanding.

Cry out for insight,

and ask for understanding.

Search for them as you would for silver;

seek them like hidden treasures.

Then you will understand what it means to fear the Lord,

and you will gain knowledge of God. (Proverbs 2:1-5 NLT).

HOW THIS PROVERB CHALLENGES ME . . .

In my PERSONAL life

In my PROFESSIONAL life

In my SPIRITUAL life

DAY THREE: "The Keys To A Wildly Successful Life"

Today May You . . . TRUST Him with everything you've got instead of TRUSTING you with everything you have, and as you live your life, TRUST His will to take you where you need to go.

Trust in the Lord with all your heart;

do not depend on your own understanding.

Seek his will in all you do,

and he will show you which path to take. (Proverbs 3:5-6 NLT).

Quality Wisdom Devotional Thought:

Christianity is best expressed when the believer is "all in." Choices, decisions, are made with a clear focus on positive action. In this instance, we see three decisive choices:

- Trust in the Lord, with all your heart (It means complete confidence in God's ability to take care of you perfectly)

- Do not depend on your own understanding (It means God has a better perspective than you do)

- Seek his will in all you do (It means you continually check in with Him about every decision you make)

- The payoff is profound: He will show you, in an obvious way, which path to take.

Turn your POSITIVE DECLARATION OF QUALITY WISDOM into this prayer of commitment:

> Lord Jesus, ***Today May I*** *TRUST You with everything I've got instead of TRUSTING me with everything I have, and as I live my life, I will TRUST Your will to take me where I need to go.*

Keys To Experiencing Quality Wisdom For Life

What do you think is the key to trusting God for His plans for you instead of trusting in your ability to create your own plans?

Going Deeper In Bible Study

*I'll give you a few prompts in **bold type** to get you started. Then you can select one or two key words, phrases or doctrines in this passage of Scripture and follow the process by going through the three key elements of doing a meaningful Bible study (Observation, Interpretation, and Application):

Trust in the Lord with all your heart;

do not depend on your own understanding.

Seek his will in all you do,

and he will show you which path to take. (Proverbs 3:5-6 NLT).

OBSERVATION: WHAT IS THE AUTHOR SAYING? {*key words, phrases or doctrines*}

INTERPRETATION: WHAT DOES IT MEAN? *{If you are doing a word study you may want to use a concordance. If you are studying a doctrine (a Biblical principle), can you give it a name? i.e., "the doctrine of . . . "}*

APPLICATION: HOW DOES IT APPLY TO ME? *{This is a key part of your Bible study. Read and pray through the Proverb again and review your thoughts on your notes on Observation and Interpretation then write out a concise personal application.}*

POSITIVE DECLARATION OF QUALITY WISDOM

Today May You . . . TRUST Him with everything you've got instead of TRUSTING you with everything you have, and as you live your life, TRUST His will to take you where you need to go.

Trust in the Lord with all your heart;

do not depend on your own understanding.

Seek his will in all you do,

and he will show you which path to take. (Proverbs 3:5-6 NLT).

HOW THIS PROVERB CHALLENGES ME . . .

In my PERSONAL life

In my PROFESSIONAL life

In my SPIRITUAL life

DAY FOUR: "Get Wisdom While You Can"

Today May You . . . GET WISDOM before foolishness gets you.

Get wisdom; develop good judgment.

Don't forget my words or turn away from them.

Don't turn your back on wisdom, for she will protect you.

Love her, and she will guard you.

Getting wisdom is the wisest thing you can do!

And whatever else you do, develop good judgment.

If you prize wisdom, she will make you great.

Embrace her, and she will honor you.

She will place a lovely wreath on your head;

she will present you with a beautiful crown." (Proverbs 4:5-9 NLT).

Quality Wisdom Devotional Thought:

The Christian life is best experienced when it is . . . *experienced*! There no such option as a passive faith for the believer who is serious about growing in faith. The very essence of Biblical faith is when action is taken. In this passage of Scripture note the ten "actions" the writer implores us to do: Get wisdom . . . Develop good judgment . . . Don't forget his words . . . Don't turn away from them . . . Don't turn your back on wisdom . . . Love her (wisdom) . . . Getting wisdom is the wisest thing you can do . . . Develop good judgement . . . Prize wisdom . . . Embrace wisdom.

So, while you have the opportunity, get wisdom before foolishness gets you.

Turn your POSITIVE DECLARATION OF QUALITY WISDOM into this prayer of commitment:

Lord Jesus, *Today May I GET WISDOM before foolishness gets me.*

Keys To Experiencing Quality Wisdom For Life

What do you think is the key to getting wisdom?

Going Deeper In Bible Study

*I'll give you a few prompts in **bold type** to get you started. Then you can select one or two key words, phrases or doctrines in this passage of Scripture and follow the process by going through the three key elements of doing a meaningful Bible study (Observation, Interpretation, and Application):

Get wisdom; develop good judgment.

Don't forget my words or turn away from them.

Don't turn your back on wisdom, for she will protect you.

Love her, and she will guard you.

Getting wisdom is the wisest thing you can do!

And whatever else you do, develop good judgment.

If you prize wisdom, she will make you great.

Embrace her, and she will honor you.

She will place a lovely wreath on your head;

she will present you with a beautiful crown." (Proverbs 4:5-9 NLT).

OBSERVATION: WHAT IS THE AUTHOR SAYING? {*key words, phrases or doctrines*}

INTERPRETATION: WHAT DOES IT MEAN? *{If you are doing a word study you may want to use a concordance. If you are studying a doctrine (a Biblical principle), can you give it a name? i.e., "the doctrine of . . . "}*

APPLICATION: HOW DOES IT APPLY TO ME? *{This is a key part of your Bible study. Read and pray through the Proverb again and review your thoughts on your notes on Observation and Interpretation then write out a concise personal application.}*

POSITIVE DECLARATION OF QUALITY WISDOM

Today May You . . . GET WISDOM before foolishness gets you.

Get wisdom; develop good judgment.

Don't forget my words or turn away from them.

Don't turn your back on wisdom, for she will protect you.

Love her, and she will guard you.

Getting wisdom is the wisest thing you can do!

And whatever else you do, develop good judgment.

If you prize wisdom, she will make you great.

Embrace her, and she will honor you.

She will place a lovely wreath on your head;

she will present you with a beautiful crown." (Proverbs 4:5-9 NLT).

HOW THIS PROVERB CHALLENGES ME . . .

In my PERSONAL life

In my PROFESSIONAL life

In my SPIRITUAL life

DAY FIVE: "Look Up Living"

Today May You . . . look UP before you look DOWN and stay out of sexual trouble.

So now, my sons, listen to me.

Never stray from what I am about to say:

Stay away from her!

Don't go near the door of her house!

If you do, you will lose your honor

and will lose to merciless people all you have achieved.

Strangers will consume your wealth,

and someone else will enjoy the fruit of your labor.

In the end you will groan in anguish

when disease consumes your body.

You will say, "How I hated discipline!

If only I had not ignored all the warnings!

Oh, why didn't I listen to my teachers?

Why didn't I pay attention to my instructors?

I have come to the brink of utter ruin,

and now I must face public disgrace." (Proverbs 5:7-14 NLT).

Quality Wisdom Devotional Thought:

Every good thing God has given to us to be enjoyed (like sex) also has the potential to be destructive IF it is used in a wrong way. Temptation is a gift if it draws us closer to the Lord. Temptation, unchecked, will pull us down into the abyss of sexual immorality. And when we are tempted and if we lose our focus upon the Lord the consequences are devastating:

- We will lose our honor
- We will lose everything we've achieved
- We will have our wealth consumed by strangers

- We will become physically sick

- We will become to the utter brink of ruin

- We will face public disgrace

But, if we look UP before we look DOWN we will stay out of sexual trouble.

Turn your POSITIVE DECLARATION OF QUALITY WISDOM into this prayer of commitment:

Lord Jesus, *Today May I LOOK UP before I LOOK DOWN so that I may STAY OUT OF TROUBLE.*

Keys To Experiencing Quality Wisdom For Life

What do you think is the key to protecting yourself to be sexually pure?

Going Deeper In Bible Study

*I'll give you a few prompts in *bold type* to get you started. Then you can select one or two key words, phrases or doctrines in this passage of Scripture and follow the process by going through the three key elements of doing a meaningful Bible study (Observation, Interpretation, and Application):

So now, my sons, listen to me.

Never stray from what I am about to say:

Stay away from her!

Don't go near the door of her house!

If you do, you will lose your honor

and will lose to merciless people all you have achieved.

Strangers will consume your wealth,

and someone else will enjoy the fruit of your labor.

In the end you will groan in anguish

when disease consumes your body.

You will say, "How I hated discipline!

If only I had not ignored all the warnings!

Oh, why didn't I listen to my teachers?

Why didn't I pay attention to my instructors?

I have come to the brink of utter ruin,

and now I must face public disgrace." (Proverbs 5:7-14 NLT).

OBSERVATION: WHAT IS THE AUTHOR SAYING? {*key words, phrases or doctrines*}

INTERPRETATION: WHAT DOES IT MEAN? {*If you are doing a word study you may want to use a concordance. If you are studying a doctrine (a Biblical principle), can you give it a name? i.e., "the doctrine of . . . "*}

APPLICATION: HOW DOES IT APPLY TO ME? {*This is a key part of your Bible study. Read and pray through the Proverb again and review your thoughts on your notes on Observation and Interpretation then write out a concise personal application.*}

POSITIVE DECLARATION OF QUALITY WISDOM

Today May You . . . look UP before you look DOWN and stay out of sexual trouble.

So now, my sons, listen to me.

Never stray from what I am about to say:

Stay away from her!

Don't go near the door of her house!

If you do, you will lose your honor

and will lose to merciless people all you have achieved.

Strangers will consume your wealth,

and someone else will enjoy the fruit of your labor.

In the end you will groan in anguish

when disease consumes your body.

You will say, "How I hated discipline!

If only I had not ignored all the warnings!

Oh, why didn't I listen to my teachers?

Why didn't I pay attention to my instructors?

I have come to the brink of utter ruin,

and now I must face public disgrace." (Proverbs 5:7-14 NLT).

HOW THIS PROVERB CHALLENGES ME . . .

In my PERSONAL life

In my PROFESSIONAL life

In my SPIRITUAL life

DAY SIX: "Embracing The Mentored Life"

Today May You . . . embrace the life teachings from your spiritual parents (Mentors) and live a life marked by success.

My son, obey your father's commands,

and don't neglect your mother's instruction.

Keep their words always in your heart.

Tie them around your neck.

When you walk, their counsel will lead you.

When you sleep, they will protect you.

When you wake up, they will advise you.

For their command is a lamp

and their instruction a light;

their corrective discipline

is the way to life. (Proverbs 6:20-23 NLT).

Quality Wisdom Devotional Thought:

Some people believe (wrongly) that experience is the best teacher. I believe it is more correct to say, *guided* experience is the best teacher. I'd much rather have someone show me the way who has already walked that path than for me go it alone and stumble on a path of hidden potholes and other unseen hazards. Note the benefits of having a quality mentor:

- When you walk, their counsel will lead you
- When you sleep, they will protect you
- When you wake up, they will advise you
- Their command is a lamp
- Their instruction is a light
- Their corrective discipline is the way to life

The payoff for those who are being mentored is to experience a life marked with success.

Turn your POSITIVE DECLARATION OF QUALITY WISDOM into this prayer of commitment:

Lord Jesus, *Today May I* embrace the life teachings from my spiritual parents (Mentors) and live a life marked by success.

Keys To Experiencing Quality Wisdom For Life

What do you think is the key to having a mentor show you how to live a successful life?

Going Deeper In Bible Study

*I'll give you a few prompts in **bold type** to get you started. Then you can select one or two key words, phrases or doctrines in this passage of Scripture and follow the process by going through the three key elements of doing a meaningful Bible study (Observation, Interpretation, and Application):

My son, obey your father's commands,

and don't neglect your mother's instruction.

Keep their words always in your heart.

Tie them around your neck.

When you walk, their counsel will lead you.

When you sleep, they will protect you.

When you wake up, they will advise you.

For their command is a lamp

and their instruction a light;

their corrective discipline

is the way to life. (Proverbs 6:20-23 NLT).

OBSERVATION: WHAT IS THE AUTHOR SAYING? *{key words, phrases or doctrines}*

INTERPRETATION: WHAT DOES IT MEAN? *{If you are doing a word study you may want to use a concordance. If you are studying a doctrine (a Biblical principle), can you give it a name? i.e., "the doctrine of . . . "}*

APPLICATION: HOW DOES IT APPLY TO ME? *{This is a key part of your Bible study. Read and pray through the Proverb again and review your thoughts on your notes on Observation and Interpretation then write out a concise personal application.}*

POSITIVE DECLARATION OF QUALITY WISDOM

Today May You . . . embrace the life teachings from your spiritual parents (Mentors) and live a life marked by success.

My son, obey your father's commands,

and don't neglect your mother's instruction.

Keep their words always in your heart.

Tie them around your neck.

When you walk, their counsel will lead you.

When you sleep, they will protect you.

When you wake up, they will advise you.

For their command is a lamp

and their instruction a light;

their corrective discipline

is the way to life. (Proverbs 6:20-23 NLT).

HOW THIS PROVERB CHALLENGES ME . . .

In my PERSONAL life

In my PROFESSIONAL life

In my SPIRITUAL life

DAY SEVEN: "The Prize-Driven Life"

Today May You . . . do whatever it takes to keep your eyes on the PRIZE of experiencing the abundant life and keep yourself from stumbling into the PIT of despair.

Follow my advice, my son;

always treasure my commands.

Obey my commands and live!

Guard my instructions as you guard your own eyes.

Tie them on your fingers as a reminder.

Write them deep within your heart. (Proverbs 7:1-3 NLT).

Quality Wisdom Devotional Thought:

Having a healthy perspective is the difference between DELIGHT and DESPAIR. There will always be a battle in our mind where an unseen tug of war is taking place between thoughts that are POSITIVE and thoughts that are NEGATIVE, thoughts that are full of DESPAIR. This passage gives us the key to experiencing the abundant life. We are to treasure God's commands and obey them. We are to internalize them (deep within out heart) for instant recall when we are in need of them for direction.

If we want the prize-driven life, then we will be willing to do whatever it takes to keep our eyes on the PRIZE of experiencing the abundant life and keep our self from stumbling into the PIT of despair.

Turn your POSITIVE DECLARATION OF QUALITY WISDOM into this prayer of commitment:

Lord Jesus, *Today May I* do whatever it takes to keep my eyes on the PRIZE of experiencing the abundant life and keep myself from stumbling into the PIT of despair.

Keys To Experiencing Quality Wisdom For Life

What do you think is the key to keeping your focus on the things that really matter?

Going Deeper In Bible Study

*I'll give you a few prompts in **bold type** to get you started. Then you can select one or two key words, phrases or doctrines in this passage of Scripture and follow the process by going through the three key elements of doing a meaningful Bible study (Observation, Interpretation, and Application):

Follow my advice, my son;

always treasure my commands.

Obey my commands and live!

Guard my instructions as you guard your own eyes.

Tie them on your fingers as a reminder.

Write them deep within your heart. (Proverbs 7:1-3 NLT).

OBSERVATION: WHAT IS THE AUTHOR SAYING? {*key words, phrases or doctrines*}

INTERPRETATION: WHAT DOES IT MEAN? *{If you are doing a word study you may want to use a concordance. If you are studying a doctrine (a Biblical principle), can you give it a name? i.e., "the doctrine of . . . "}*

APPLICATION: HOW DOES IT APPLY TO ME? *{This is a key part of your Bible study. Read and pray through the Proverb again and review your thoughts on your notes on Observation and Interpretation then write out a concise personal application.}*

POSITIVE DECLARATION OF QUALITY WISDOM

Today May You . . . do whatever it takes to keep your eyes on the PRIZE of experiencing the abundant life and keep yourself from stumbling into the PIT of despair.

Follow my advice, my son;

always treasure my commands.

Obey my commands and live!

Guard my instructions as you guard your own eyes.

Tie them on your fingers as a reminder.

Write them deep within your heart. (Proverbs 7:1-3 NLT).

HOW THIS PROVERB CHALLENGES ME . . .

In my PERSONAL life

In my PROFESSIONAL life

In my SPIRITUAL life

DAY EIGHT: "Wisdom Matters"

Today May You . . . cling to every bit of wisdom you can collect . . . and use it.

My advice is wholesome.

There is nothing devious or crooked in it.

My words are plain to anyone with understanding,

clear to those with knowledge.

Choose my instruction rather than silver,

and knowledge rather than pure gold.

For wisdom is far more valuable than rubies.

Nothing you desire can compare with it. (Proverbs 8:8-11 NLT).

Quality Wisdom Devotional Thought:

Are you a "collector?" Some collect unique coins; others may collect old books. But there is something much more valuable to collect than rare coins and ancient manuscripts. These are temporal. There is another precious possession that is eternal. The writer of Proverbs says its wisdom and is more valuable than anything you can collect in this life. In his own words:

- Choose my instruction rather than silver and knowledge rather than pure gold
- For wisdom is far more valuable than rubies. Nothing you desire can compare with it

If you want to experience transformational growth in your life, cling to every bit of wisdom you can collect . . . and use it.

Turn your POSITIVE DECLARATION OF QUALITY WISDOM into this prayer of commitment:

Lord Jesus, *Today May I* cling to every bit of wisdom I can collect . . . and use it.

Keys To Experiencing Quality Wisdom For Life

What do you think is the key to placing a value on wisdom?

Going Deeper In Bible Study

*I'll give you a few prompts in **bold type** to get you started. Then you can select one or two key words, phrases or doctrines in this passage of Scripture and follow the process by going through the three key elements of doing a meaningful Bible study (Observation, Interpretation, and Application):

My advice is wholesome.

There is nothing devious or crooked in it.

My words are plain to anyone with understanding,

clear to those with knowledge.

Choose my instruction rather than silver,

and knowledge rather than pure gold.

For wisdom is far more valuable than rubies.

Nothing you desire can compare with it. (Proverbs 8:8-11 NLT).

OBSERVATION: WHAT IS THE AUTHOR SAYING? {*key words, phrases or doctrines*}

INTERPRETATION: WHAT DOES IT MEAN? *{If you are doing a word study you may want to use a concordance. If you are studying a doctrine (a Biblical principle), can you give it a name? i.e., "the doctrine of . . . "}*

APPLICATION: HOW DOES IT APPLY TO ME? *{This is a key part of your Bible study. Read and pray through the Proverb again and review your thoughts on your notes on Observation and Interpretation then write out a concise personal application.}*

POSITIVE DECLARATION OF QUALITY WISDOM

Today May You . . . cling to every bit of wisdom you can collect . . . and use it.

My advice is wholesome.

There is nothing devious or crooked in it.

My words are plain to anyone with understanding,

clear to those with knowledge.

Choose my instruction rather than silver,

and knowledge rather than pure gold.

For wisdom is far more valuable than rubies.

Nothing you desire can compare with it. (Proverbs 8:8-11 NLT).

HOW THIS PROVERB CHALLENGES ME . . .

In my PERSONAL life

In my PROFESSIONAL life

In my SPIRITUAL life

DAY NINE: "Time Investment"

Today May You . . . make an intentional investment in people who are serious about becoming an even better version of themselves.

Anyone who rebukes a mocker will get an insult in return.

Anyone who corrects the wicked will get hurt.

So don't bother correcting mockers;

they will only hate you.

But correct the wise,

and they will love you.

Instruct the wise,

and they will be even wiser.

Teach the righteous,

and they will learn even more. (Proverbs 9:7-9 NLT).

Quality Wisdom Devotional Thought:

Most likely, someone you know showed you how to become a better version of yourself. They are called "teachers," "guides," and "mentors." The Biblical term is "discipleship." Time is one of the greatest commodities we can possess. How we spend it is a call to stewardship. We are warned not to waste it on the wrong people. When we invest our time in the "right" people the blessings are many:

- Correct the wise, and they will love you.
- Instruct the wise, and they will be even wiser.
- Teach the righteous, and they will learn even more.

When we make an intentional investment in people who are serious about becoming an even better version of themselves, we give glory to God and good to them.

Turn your POSITIVE DECLARATION OF QUALITY WISDOM into this prayer of commitment:

Lord Jesus, *Today May I* make an intentional investment in people who are serious about becoming an even better version of themselves.

Keys To Experiencing Quality Wisdom For Life

What do you think is the key to knowing how to invest your time in the right person?

Going Deeper In Bible Study

*I'll give you a few prompts in **bold type** to get you started. Then you can select one or two key words, phrases or doctrines in this passage of Scripture and follow the process by going through the three key elements of doing a meaningful Bible study (Observation, Interpretation, and Application):

Anyone who rebukes a mocker will get an insult in return.

Anyone who corrects the wicked will get hurt.

So don't bother correcting mockers;

they will only hate you.

But correct the wise,

and they will love you.

Instruct the wise,

and they will be even wiser.

Teach the righteous,

and they will learn even more. (Proverbs 9:7-9 NLT).

OBSERVATION: WHAT IS THE AUTHOR SAYING? {*key words, phrases or doctrines*}

INTERPRETATION: WHAT DOES IT MEAN? *{If you are doing a word study you may want to use a concordance. If you are studying a doctrine (a Biblical principle), can you give it a name? i.e., "the doctrine of . . . "}*

APPLICATION: HOW DOES IT APPLY TO ME? *{This is a key part of your Bible study. Read and pray through the Proverb again and review your thoughts on your notes on Observation and Interpretation then write out a concise personal application.}*

POSITIVE DECLARATION OF QUALITY WISDOM

Today May You . . . make an intentional investment in people who are serious about becoming an even better version of themselves.

Anyone who rebukes a mocker will get an insult in return.

Anyone who corrects the wicked will get hurt.

So don't bother correcting mockers;

they will only hate you.

But correct the wise,

and they will love you.

Instruct the wise,

and they will be even wiser.

Teach the righteous,

and they will learn even more. (Proverbs 9:7-9 NLT).

HOW THIS PROVERB CHALLENGES ME . . .

In my PERSONAL life

In my PROFESSIONAL life

In my SPIRITUAL life

DAY TEN: "Business Issues"

Today May You . . . make it your goal not to be a "Christian" businessman or businesswoman but to be a businessman or businesswoman who TRUSTS God, who LIVES for God, who LOVES like God, and who is BLESSED by God.

Tainted wealth has no lasting value,

but right living can save your life. (Proverbs 10:2 NLT).

Quality Wisdom Devotional Thought:

BELIEF. IDENTITY. PRACTICE. What we believe usually forms who we are and who we are often dictates what we do. These three components are our guide on how we treat others. This Proverb is clear in showing the great contrasts between right and wrong values.

- Tainted wealth has no lasting value—The love of money is the root of all evil and doing evil things to get it at any and all costs is an evil value.
- Right living can save your life—It's never wrong to do it the right way.

Committing to do business by "The Book" will not only add value to others but will add value to ourselves too.

Turn your POSITIVE DECLARATION OF QUALITY WISDOM into this prayer of commitment:

Lord Jesus, *Today May I* make it my goal not to be a "Christian" businessman or businesswoman but to be a businessman or businesswoman who TRUSTS God, who LIVES for God, who LOVES like God, and who is BLESSED by God.

Keys To Experiencing Quality Wisdom For Life

What do you think is the key to earning a living the right way?

Going Deeper In Bible Study

*I'll give you a few prompts in **bold type** to get you started. Then you can select one or two key words, phrases or doctrines in this passage of Scripture and follow the process by going through the three key elements of doing a meaningful Bible study (Observation, Interpretation, and Application):

Tainted wealth has no lasting value,
but right living can save your life. (Proverbs 10:2 NLT).

OBSERVATION: WHAT IS THE AUTHOR SAYING? {*key words, phrases or doctrines*}

INTERPRETATION: WHAT DOES IT MEAN? *{If you are doing a word study you may want to use a concordance. If you are studying a doctrine (a Biblical principle), can you give it a name? i.e., "the doctrine of . . . "}*

APPLICATION: HOW DOES IT APPLY TO ME? *{This is a key part of your Bible study. Read and pray through the Proverb again and review your thoughts on your notes on Observation and Interpretation then write out a concise personal application.}*

POSITIVE DECLARATION OF QUALITY WISDOM

Today May You . . . make it your goal not to be a "Christian" businessman or businesswoman but to be a businessman or businesswoman who TRUSTS God, who LIVES for God, who LOVES like God, and who is BLESSED by God.

Tainted wealth has no lasting value,

but right living can save your life. (Proverbs 10:2 NLT).

HOW THIS PROVERB CHALLENGES ME . . .

In my PERSONAL life

In my PROFESSIONAL life

In my SPIRITUAL life

DAY ELEVEN: "God's GPS For You"

Today May You . . . make sure your moral compass is true in every business and personal relationship transaction you make.

The Lord detests the use of dishonest scales,

but he delights in accurate weights. (Proverbs 11:1 NLT).

Quality Wisdom Devotional Thought:

One of the best indicators of one's character is to make an intentional decision when no one else is looking (and not worry about it). Honest people act honestly no matter the circumstance; no matter who is or who is not looking over their shoulder. The characteristic of honesty builds up over time. The more it's practiced, the better we become in being honest. Honestly, the Lord wants us to excel in honesty. The contrast is stark between what the Lord likes and dislikes.

- He *DETESTS* the use of dishonest scales
- He *DELIGHTS* in accurate weights

If you really want to experience a quality life, then you've got to make sure your moral compass is true in every business and personal relationship you make.

Turn your POSITIVE DECLARATION OF QUALITY WISDOM into this prayer of commitment:

Lord Jesus, *Today May I* make sure my moral compass is true in every business and personal relationship transaction I make.

Keys To Experiencing Quality Wisdom For Life

What do you think is the key to living by a moral compass?

Going Deeper In Bible Study

*I'll give you a few prompts in **bold type** to get you started. Then you can select one or two key words, phrases or doctrines in this passage of Scripture and follow the process by going through the three key elements of doing a meaningful Bible study (Observation, Interpretation, and Application):

The Lord detests the use of dishonest scales,
but he delights in accurate weights. (Proverbs 11:1 NLT).

OBSERVATION: WHAT IS THE AUTHOR SAYING? *{key words, phrases or doctrines}*

INTERPRETATION: WHAT DOES IT MEAN? *{If you are doing a word study you may want to use a concordance. If you are studying a doctrine (a Biblical principle), can you give it a name? i.e., "the doctrine of . . . "}*

APPLICATION: HOW DOES IT APPLY TO ME? *{This is a key part of your Bible study. Read and pray through the Proverb again and review your thoughts on your notes on Observation and Interpretation then write out a concise personal application.}*

POSITIVE DECLARATION OF QUALITY WISDOM

Today May You . . . make sure your moral compass is true in every business and personal relationship transaction you make.

The Lord detests the use of dishonest scales,

but he delights in accurate weights. (Proverbs 11:1 NLT).

HOW THIS PROVERB CHALLENGES ME . . .

In my PERSONAL life

In my PROFESSIONAL life

In my SPIRITUAL life

DAY TWELVE: "Love What Matters"

Today May You . . . LOVE humility so that you may embrace discipline and correction and LEARN.

To learn, you must love discipline;

it is stupid to hate correction. (Proverbs 12:1 NLT).

Quality Wisdom Devotional Thought:

What we love will largely determine what we do and how we do it. There are some people who do just enough to get by. For them, short cuts are always the first option, but not the best choice. What they "shun," they so desperately need. We need to love what matters and be open to a healthy, honest critique of our life.

- We need to learn; we need to love discipline.
- We need to not be stupid and hate correction.

If you want to grow as an individual, then you will have to love humility so that you may embrace discipline and correction and learn.

Turn your POSITIVE DECLARATION OF QUALITY WISDOM into this prayer of commitment:

Lord Jesus, *Today May I* LOVE humility so that I may embrace discipline and correction and LEARN.

Keys To Experiencing Quality Wisdom For Life

What do you think is the key to loving correction?

Going Deeper In Bible Study

*I'll give you a few prompts in **bold type** to get you started. Then you can select one or two key words, phrases or doctrines in this passage of Scripture and follow the process by going through the three key elements of doing a meaningful Bible study (Observation, Interpretation, and Application):

To learn, you must love discipline;
it is stupid to hate correction. (Proverbs 12:1 NLT).

OBSERVATION: WHAT IS THE AUTHOR SAYING? *{key words, phrases or doctrines}*

INTERPRETATION: WHAT DOES IT MEAN? *{If you are doing a word study you may want to use a concordance. If you are studying a doctrine (a Biblical principle), can you give it a name? i.e., "the doctrine of . . . "}*

APPLICATION: HOW DOES IT APPLY TO ME? *{This is a key part of your Bible study. Read and pray through the Proverb again and review your thoughts on your notes on Observation and Interpretation then write out a concise personal application.}*

POSITIVE DECLARATION OF QUALITY WISDOM

Today May You . . . LOVE humility so that you may embrace discipline and correction and LEARN.

To learn, you must love discipline;

it is stupid to hate correction. (Proverbs 12:1 NLT).

HOW THIS PROVERB CHALLENGES ME . . .

In my PERSONAL life

In my PROFESSIONAL life

In my SPIRITUAL life

DAY THIRTEEN: "Tongue Twisters"

Today May You . . . watch what you say so you will not have to eat your words.

Those who control their tongue will have a long life;

opening your mouth can ruin everything. (Proverbs 13:3 NLT).

Quality Wisdom Devotional Thought:

Have you ever thought how words "taste?" I'm pretty sure that the destructive ones that begin in our mind but are NOT allowed to escape through our mouth taste pretty good. The toxic ones are the words that are marinated in a bitter sauce and then are injected in someone's heart. There are clear consequences (good and bad) when it comes to the power of words.

- Those who control their tongue will have a long life (the good consequence)
- Opening your mouth can ruin everything (the bad consequence)

Because we are "human" there will always be a struggle with our tongue, real tongue twisters. But if we watch what we say we will not have to eat our own words.

Turn your POSITIVE DECLARATION OF QUALITY WISDOM into this prayer of commitment:

Lord Jesus, *Today May I* watch what I say so I will not have to eat my words.

Keys To Experiencing Quality Wisdom For Life

What do you think is the key to controlling what comes out of your mouth?

Going Deeper In Bible Study

*I'll give you a few prompts in **bold type** to get you started. Then you can select one or two key words, phrases or doctrines in this passage of Scripture and follow the process by going through the three key elements of doing a meaningful Bible study (Observation, Interpretation, and Application):

Those who control their tongue will have a long life;
opening your mouth can ruin everything. (Proverbs 13:3 NLT).

OBSERVATION: WHAT IS THE AUTHOR SAYING? {*key words, phrases or doctrines*}

INTERPRETATION: WHAT DOES IT MEAN? {*If you are doing a word study you may want to use a concordance. If you are studying a doctrine (a Biblical principle), can you give it a name? i.e., "the doctrine of . . . "*}

APPLICATION: HOW DOES IT APPLY TO ME? {*This is a key part of your Bible study. Read and pray through the Proverb again and review your thoughts on your notes on Observation and Interpretation then write out a concise personal application.*}

POSITIVE DECLARATION OF QUALITY WISDOM

Today May You . . . watch what you say so you will not have to eat your words.

Those who control their tongue will have a long life;

opening your mouth can ruin everything. (Proverbs 13:3 NLT).

HOW THIS PROVERB CHALLENGES ME . . .

In my PERSONAL life

In my PROFESSIONAL life

In my SPIRITUAL life

DAY FOURTEEN: "Right On!"

Today May You . . . make decisions that keep you on the RIGHT path, connect you with the RIGHT people, and help you wind up in the RIGHT place.

Those who follow the right path fear the Lord;
those who take the wrong path despise him. (Proverbs 14:2 NLT).

Quality Wisdom Devotional Thought:

One of the most important decisions we will ever make is the choices we implement not to only find the right path but to also have the discipline to stay on it. Do we have any resources available to us that will make life go right? The writer of the Proverb offers one key.

- Those who follow the right path fear the Lord. What does it mean to "fear the Lord?" It means we are to have an awesome reverence, an awesome respect and love for Him. This is in great contrast with this dire warning:

- Those who take the wrong path despise him. It can also be stated another way: choosing the wrong path is a heart condition that reveals an attitude of spite.

It is essential that you make decisions that keep you on the RIGHT path, connect you with the RIGHT people, and help you wind up in the RIGHT place.

Turn your POSITIVE DECLARATION OF QUALITY WISDOM into this prayer of commitment:

Lord Jesus, *Today May I* make decisions that keep me on the RIGHT path, connecting me with the RIGHT people, and help me wind up in the RIGHT place.

Keys To Experiencing Quality Wisdom For Life

What do you think is the key to making sure you live on the right path?

Going Deeper In Bible Study

*I'll give you a few prompts in **bold type** to get you started. Then you can select one or two key words, phrases or doctrines in this passage of Scripture and follow the process by going through the three key elements of doing a meaningful Bible study (Observation, Interpretation, and Application):

Those who follow the right path fear the Lord;
those who take the wrong path despise him. (Proverbs 14:2 NLT).

OBSERVATION: WHAT IS THE AUTHOR SAYING? {*key words, phrases or doctrines*}

INTERPRETATION: WHAT DOES IT MEAN? *{If you are doing a word study you may want to use a concordance. If you are studying a doctrine (a Biblical principle), can you give it a name? i.e., "the doctrine of . . . "}*

APPLICATION: HOW DOES IT APPLY TO ME? *{This is a key part of your Bible study. Read and pray through the Proverb again and review your thoughts on your notes on Observation and Interpretation then write out a concise personal application.}*

POSITIVE DECLARATION OF QUALITY WISDOM

Today May You . . . make decisions that keep you on the RIGHT path, connect you with the RIGHT people, and help you wind up in the RIGHT place.

Those who follow the right path fear the Lord;

those who take the wrong path despise him. (Proverbs 14:2 NLT).

HOW THIS PROVERB CHALLENGES ME . . .

In my PERSONAL life

In my PROFESSIONAL life

In my SPIRITUAL life

DAY FIFTEEN: "Word Diplomat"

Today May You . . . WATCH what you say, WHO you say it to, and HOW you say it.

A gentle answer deflects anger,

but harsh words make tempers flare.

The tongue of the wise makes knowledge appealing,

but the mouth of a fool belches out foolishness. (Proverbs 15:1-2 NLT).

Quality Wisdom Devotional Thought:

Word stewardship. Exactly what is it and why is it so important? Word stewardship is being wise on how you "spend" your words. The right words spent in the right way becomes a great investment.

- A gentle answer deflects anger
- The tongue of the wise makes knowledge appealing

On the other hand,

- harsh words make tempers flare
- the mouth of a fool belches out foolishness

The essential challenge for every believer is to WATCH what you say, WHO you say it to, and HOW you say it.

Turn your POSITIVE DECLARATION OF QUALITY WISDOM into this prayer of commitment:

Lord Jesus, *Today May I* WATCH what I say, WHO I say it to, and HOW I say it.

Keys To Experiencing Quality Wisdom For Life

What do you think is the key to using your words for blessing and not for cursing?

Going Deeper In Bible Study

*I'll give you a few prompts in **bold type** to get you started. Then you can select one or two key words, phrases or doctrines in this passage of Scripture and follow the process by going through the three key elements of doing a meaningful Bible study (Observation, Interpretation, and Application):

A gentle answer deflects anger,
but harsh words make tempers flare.
The tongue of the wise makes knowledge appealing,
but the mouth of a fool belches out foolishness. (Proverbs 15:1-2 NLT).

OBSERVATION: WHAT IS THE AUTHOR SAYING? {*key words, phrases or doctrines*}

INTERPRETATION: WHAT DOES IT MEAN? *{If you are doing a word study you may want to use a concordance. If you are studying a doctrine (a Biblical principle), can you give it a name? i.e., "the doctrine of . . . "}*

APPLICATION: HOW DOES IT APPLY TO ME? *{This is a key part of your Bible study. Read and pray through the Proverb again and review your thoughts on your notes on Observation and Interpretation then write out a concise personal application.}*

POSITIVE DECLARATION OF QUALITY WISDOM

Today May You . . . WATCH what you say, WHO you say it to, and HOW you say it.

A gentle answer deflects anger,

but harsh words make tempers flare.

The tongue of the wise makes knowledge appealing,

but the mouth of a fool belches out foolishness. (Proverbs 15:1-2 NLT).

HOW THIS PROVERB CHALLENGES ME . . .

In my PERSONAL life

In my PROFESSIONAL life

In my SPIRITUAL life

DAY SIXTEEN: "No Limit To Your Dreams"

Today May You . . . be free to dream a dream that only God can fulfill.

We can make our own plans,

but the Lord gives the right answer. (Proverbs 16:1 NLT).

Quality Wisdom Devotional Thought:

Big dreams. Big plans. Big ideas. It's a wonderful thing to have big dreams, plans, and ideas; especially when the Lord gives them to us. How do we know if we are the creator of big dreams, plan, and ideas or is the Lord behind them? Sometimes we won't know until we try. This proverb is a wonderful template on the blessing of being able to make our plans. It's okay, as long as we stay flexible, submit our plans to Him and are willing for His will.

- We can make our own plans
- The Lord gives the right answer

Big dreams, submitted an even bigger God, creates a big life. The Lord wants you to be free to dream a dream that only God can fulfill.

Turn your POSITIVE DECLARATION OF QUALITY WISDOM into this prayer of commitment:

Lord Jesus, *Today May I* be free to dream a dream that only God can fulfill.

Keys To Experiencing Quality Wisdom For Life

What do you think is the key to giving your plans for the Lord?

Going Deeper In Bible Study

*I'll give you a few prompts in **bold type** to get you started. Then you can select one or two key words, phrases or doctrines in this passage of Scripture and follow the process by going through the three key elements of doing a meaningful Bible study (Observation, Interpretation, and Application):

We can make our own plans,
but the Lord gives the right answer. (Proverbs 16:1 NLT).

OBSERVATION: WHAT IS THE AUTHOR SAYING? *{key words, phrases or doctrines}*

INTERPRETATION: WHAT DOES IT MEAN? *{If you are doing a word study you may want to use a concordance. If you are studying a doctrine (a Biblical principle), can you give it a name? i.e., "the doctrine of . . ."}*

APPLICATION: HOW DOES IT APPLY TO ME? *{This is a key part of your Bible study. Read and pray through the Proverb again and review your thoughts on your notes on Observation and Interpretation then write out a concise personal application.}*

POSITIVE DECLARATION OF QUALITY WISDOM

Today May You . . . WATCH what you say, WHO you say it to, and HOW you say it.

We can make our own plans,

but the Lord gives the right answer. (Proverbs 16:1 NLT).

HOW THIS PROVERB CHALLENGES ME . . .

In my PERSONAL life

In my PROFESSIONAL life

In my SPIRITUAL life

DAY SEVENTEEN: "Heart Check"

Today May You . . . keep your integrity in what you think and in what you say and in what you do.

Fire tests the purity of silver and gold,

but the Lord tests the heart. (Proverbs 17:3 NLT).

Quality Wisdom Devotional Thought:

It has been said that God is far more concerned about our character than He is about our comfort. One of the best ways to find out what we are made of is not during times of comfort but when we are tested. Instead of dreading the test, we should grateful for it. The question is this: do we trust God with our heart? He, and He alone, is worthy to test our heart. Remember,

Fire tests the purity of silver and gold, but the Lord tests the heart. And when He does a heart check on you, will be able to keep your integrity in what you think and in what you say and in what you do.

Turn your POSITIVE DECLARATION OF QUALITY WISDOM into this prayer of commitment:

Lord Jesus, *Today May I* keep my integrity in what I think and in what I say and in what I do.

Keys To Experiencing Quality Wisdom For Life

What do you think is the key to keeping your integrity intact?

Going Deeper In Bible Study

*I'll give you a few prompts in **bold type** to get you started. Then you can select one or two key words, phrases or doctrines in this passage of Scripture and follow the process by going through the three key elements of doing a meaningful Bible study (Observation, Interpretation, and Application):

Fire tests the purity of silver and gold,
but the Lord tests the heart. (Proverbs 17:3 NLT).

OBSERVATION: WHAT IS THE AUTHOR SAYING? {*key words, phrases or doctrines*}

INTERPRETATION: WHAT DOES IT MEAN? {*If you are doing a word study you may want to use a concordance. If you are studying a doctrine (a Biblical principle), can you give it a name? i.e., "the doctrine of . . . "*}

APPLICATION: HOW DOES IT APPLY TO ME? {*This is a key part of your Bible study. Read and pray through the Proverb again and review your thoughts on your notes on Observation and Interpretation then write out a concise personal application.*}

POSITIVE DECLARATION OF QUALITY WISDOM

Today May You . . . keep your integrity in what you think and in what you say and in what you do.

Fire tests the purity of silver and gold,

but the Lord tests the heart. (Proverbs 17:3 NLT).

HOW THIS PROVERB CHALLENGES ME . . .

In my PERSONAL life

In my PROFESSIONAL life

In my SPIRITUAL life

DAY EIGHTEEN: "Wisdom Source"

Today May You . . . be a plentiful resource of wisdom that wisdom hunters can come and draw from you.

Wise words are like deep waters;

wisdom flows from the wise like a bubbling brook. (Proverbs 18:4 NLT).

Quality Wisdom Devotional Thought:

The Lord has created us for two reasons: to glorify Him and then to be a blessing to others. One way we can be a blessing to others is to become people of wisdom. How do we become a plentiful resource of wisdom that wisdom hunters can come and draw from us? We go to the SOURCE of Wisdom and learn from Him. Once we are filled by the Lord, we will have plenty of wise words to share with those we can add value to and influence. This is exactly what the writer of this Proverb shares:

- Wise words are like deep waters
- Wisdom flows from the wise like a bubbling brook

Turn your POSITIVE DECLARATION OF QUALITY WISDOM into this prayer of commitment:

Lord Jesus, *Today May I* be a plentiful resource of wisdom that wisdom hunters can come and draw from me.

Keys To Experiencing Quality Wisdom For Life

What do you think is the key to becoming a reliable resource for wisdom?

Going Deeper In Bible Study

*I'll give you a few prompts in **bold type** to get you started. Then you can select one or two key words, phrases or doctrines in this passage of Scripture and follow the process by going through the three key elements of doing a meaningful Bible study (Observation, Interpretation, and Application):

Wise words are like deep waters;
wisdom flows from the wise like a bubbling brook. (Proverbs 18:4 NLT).

OBSERVATION: WHAT IS THE AUTHOR SAYING? {*key words, phrases or doctrines*}

INTERPRETATION: WHAT DOES IT MEAN? {*If you are doing a word study you may want to use a concordance. If you are studying a doctrine (a Biblical principle), can you give it a name? i.e., "the doctrine of . . . "}*

APPLICATION: HOW DOES IT APPLY TO ME? {*This is a key part of your Bible study. Read and pray through the Proverb again and review your thoughts on your notes on Observation and Interpretation then write out a concise personal application.}*

POSITIVE DECLARATION OF QUALITY WISDOM

Today May You . . . be a plentiful resource of wisdom that wisdom hunters can come and draw from you.

Wise words are like deep waters;

wisdom flows from the wise like a bubbling brook. (Proverbs 18:4 NLT).

HOW THIS PROVERB CHALLENGES ME . . .

In my PERSONAL life

In my PROFESSIONAL life

In my SPIRITUAL life

DAY NINTEEN: "got Honesty?"

Today May You . . . be HONEST with others, HONEST with yourself, and HONEST to God.

Better to be poor and honest

than to be dishonest and a fool. (Proverbs 19:1 NLT).

Quality Wisdom Devotional Thought:

Money matters. Of course, it does. But the love of it? Scripture warns against it (see 1 Timothy 6:10). Like an addictive serum, the pursuit of wealth for all of the wrong reasons and in all of the wrong ways can make fools out of all of us. Honesty is a desired treasure. The writer of Proverbs is candid when he declares,

Better to be poor and honest than to be dishonest and a fool. No serious follower of Jesus wants to be known as a dishonest fool. Those who desire to live a wildly successful life is willing to be HONEST with others, HONEST with themselves, and HONEST to God.

Turn your POSITIVE DECLARATION OF QUALITY WISDOM into this prayer of commitment:

Lord Jesus, *Today May I* be HONEST with others, HONEST with myself, and HONEST to God.

Keys To Experiencing Quality Wisdom For Life

What do you think is the key to being honest with others, with yourself, and honest to God?

Going Deeper In Bible Study

*I'll give you a few prompts in **bold type** to get you started. Then you can select one or two key words, phrases or doctrines in this passage of Scripture and follow the process by going through the three key elements of doing a meaningful Bible study (Observation, Interpretation, and Application):

Better to be poor and honest
than to be dishonest and a fool. (Proverbs 19:1 NLT).

OBSERVATION: WHAT IS THE AUTHOR SAYING? {*key words, phrases or doctrines*}

INTERPRETATION: WHAT DOES IT MEAN? {*If you are doing a word study you may want to use a concordance. If you are studying a doctrine (a Biblical principle), can you give it a name? i.e., "the doctrine of . . . "*}

APPLICATION: HOW DOES IT APPLY TO ME? {*This is a key part of your Bible study. Read and pray through the Proverb again and review your thoughts on your notes on Observation and Interpretation then write out a concise personal application.*}

POSITIVE DECLARATION OF QUALITY WISDOM

Today May You . . . be HONEST with others, HONEST with yourself, and HONEST to God.

Better to be poor and honest

than to be dishonest and a fool. (Proverbs 19:1 NLT).

HOW THIS PROVERB CHALLENGES ME . . .

In my PERSONAL life

In my PROFESSIONAL life

In my SPIRITUAL life

DAY TWENTY: "Focused Living"

Today May You . . . take the HIGH road and walk over those who are UNDER the road.

Avoiding a fight is a mark of honor;

only fools insist on quarreling. (Proverbs 20:3 NLT).

Quality Wisdom Devotional Thought:

You probably have heard the saying, "It's better to lose the battle instead of losing the war." It means, we need to learn when to fight the battle and when it's best to just concede and step away. We live in a "I want to be proven right" kind of world and will do anything to prove it, even at the expense of bringing unrepairable harm to a relationship and destroying one's personal testimony. It takes a person who is comfortable in their own skin to resist the urge to join a fight that is not worth the time and effort. The writer of Proverbs is crystal clear in describing what kind of person God wants us to be:

- Avoiding a fight is a mark of honor; only fools insist on quarreling.
- Or in other words, we are to take the HIGH road and walk over those who are UNDER the road

Turn your POSITIVE DECLARATION OF QUALITY WISDOM into this prayer of commitment:

Lord Jesus, *Today May I* take the HIGH road and walk over those who are UNDER the road.

Keys To Experiencing Quality Wisdom For Life

What do you think is the key to living above the fray?

Going Deeper In Bible Study

*I'll give you a few prompts in **bold type** to get you started. Then you can select one or two key words, phrases or doctrines in this passage of Scripture and follow the process by going through the three key elements of doing a meaningful Bible study (Observation, Interpretation, and Application):

Avoiding a fight is a mark of honor;
only fools insist on quarreling. (Proverbs 20:3 NLT).

OBSERVATION: WHAT IS THE AUTHOR SAYING? {*key words, phrases or doctrines*}

INTERPRETATION: WHAT DOES IT MEAN? {*If you are doing a word study you may want to use a concordance. If you are studying a doctrine (a Biblical principle), can you give it a name? i.e., "the doctrine of . . . "*}

APPLICATION: HOW DOES IT APPLY TO ME? {*This is a key part of your Bible study. Read and pray through the Proverb again and review your thoughts on your notes on Observation and Interpretation then write out a concise personal application.*}

POSITIVE DECLARATION OF QUALITY WISDOM

Today May You . . . take the HIGH road and walk over those who are UNDER the road.

Avoiding a fight is a mark of honor;

only fools insist on quarreling. (Proverbs 20:3 NLT).

HOW THIS PROVERB CHALLENGES ME . . .

In my PERSONAL life

In my PROFESSIONAL life

In my SPIRITUAL life

DAY TWENTY-ONE: "Heart Check"

Today May You . . . check your HEART before you trust your EYES.

People may be right in their own eyes,

but the Lord examines their heart. (Proverbs 21:2 NLT).

Quality Wisdom Devotional Thought:

It seems our vision is much sharper when our view is seen through the eyes of the Lord. We may experience many occasions when it seems everything looks to be right on, from our perspective. And as right as we may think we are, because we are human, we can be right but be absolutely wrong. We must be humble enough to have a tender heart that wants His way and not ours. What is the principle here in this Proverb?

- People may be right in their own eyes (and that is a normal human response)
- but the Lord examines their heart (and that is a supernatural resource)

If we desire to grow in wisdom, we need to check our heart before we trust our eyes.

Turn your POSITIVE DECLARATION OF QUALITY WISDOM into this prayer of commitment:

Lord Jesus, *Today May I* check my HEART before I trust my EYES.

Keys To Experiencing Quality Wisdom For Life

What do you think is the key to not assuming you know God's plan before you know it?

Going Deeper In Bible Study

*I'll give you a few prompts in **bold type** to get you started. Then you can select one or two key words, phrases or doctrines in this passage of Scripture and follow the process by going through the three key elements of doing a meaningful Bible study (Observation, Interpretation, and Application):

People may be right in their own eyes,
but the Lord examines their heart. (Proverbs 21:2 NLT).

OBSERVATION: WHAT IS THE AUTHOR SAYING? {*key words, phrases or doctrines*}

INTERPRETATION: WHAT DOES IT MEAN? {*If you are doing a word study you may want to use a concordance. If you are studying a doctrine (a Biblical principle), can you give it a name? i.e., "the doctrine of . . . "*}

APPLICATION: HOW DOES IT APPLY TO ME? {*This is a key part of your Bible study. Read and pray through the Proverb again and review your thoughts on your notes on Observation and Interpretation then write out a concise personal application.*}

POSITIVE DECLARATION OF QUALITY WISDOM

Today May You . . . check your HEART before you trust your EYES.

People may be right in their own eyes,

but the Lord examines their heart. (Proverbs 21:2 NLT).

HOW THIS PROVERB CHALLENGES ME . . .

In my PERSONAL life

In my PROFESSIONAL life

In my SPIRITUAL life

DAY TWENTY-TWO: "Character Vs. Comfort"

Today May You . . . live like CHARACTER matters more than your material COMFORT.

Choose a good reputation over great riches;
being held in high esteem is better than silver or gold. (Proverbs 22:1 NLT).

Quality Wisdom Devotional Thought:

A life of legacy is not an overnight occurrence. It takes years . . .

- Of right thinking

- Of right choices

- Of right living

It takes years to create a lasting legacy. The wrong kind of thinking, wrong choices, and wrong living can destroy it in a moment. That is why the writer of this Proverb was so adamant to record these words to us:

- Choose a good reputation over great riches; (notice the power of the choice here)

- being held in high esteem is better than silver or gold. (what we value the most matters in the long-term)

When we choose to value character over comfort, we are well on the way to experiencing a life of transformational wisdom.

Turn your POSITIVE DECLARATION OF QUALITY WISDOM into this prayer of commitment:

Lord Jesus, *Today May I* live like CHARACTER matters more than my material COMFORT.

Keys To Experiencing Quality Wisdom For Life

What do you think is the key to developing good character?

Going Deeper In Bible Study

*I'll give you a few prompts in **bold type** to get you started. Then you can select one or two key words, phrases or doctrines in this passage of Scripture and follow the process by going through the three key elements of doing a meaningful Bible study (Observation, Interpretation, and Application):

Choose a good reputation over great riches;
being held in high esteem is better than silver or gold. (Proverbs 22:1 NLT).

OBSERVATION: WHAT IS THE AUTHOR SAYING? {*key words, phrases or doctrines*}

INTERPRETATION: WHAT DOES IT MEAN? *{If you are doing a word study you may want to use a concordance. If you are studying a doctrine (a Biblical principle), can you give it a name? i.e., "the doctrine of . . . "}*

APPLICATION: HOW DOES IT APPLY TO ME? *{This is a key part of your Bible study. Read and pray through the Proverb again and review your thoughts on your notes on Observation and Interpretation then write out a concise personal application.}*

POSITIVE DECLARATION OF QUALITY WISDOM

Today May You . . . live like CHARACTER matters more than your material COMFORT.

Choose a good reputation over great riches;

being held in high esteem is better than silver or gold. (Proverbs 22:1 NLT).

HOW THIS PROVERB CHALLENGES ME . . .

In my PERSONAL life

In my PROFESSIONAL life

In my SPIRITUAL life

DAY TWENTY-THREE: "Jehovah Jireh, My Provider"

Today May You . . . TRUST GOD FOR WHAT YOU NEED and then allow Him, in His way, to PROVIDE ALL OF YOUR NEEDS.

Don't wear yourself out trying to get rich. Be wise enough to know when to quit. In the blink of an eye wealth disappears, for it will sprout wings and fly away like an eagle. (Proverbs 23:4-5 NLT).

Quality Wisdom Devotional Thought:

It has been said that "time" is money and there may be some truth to that statement. But how much money is enough? And how much time is enough when it's devoted to make money? If all of a person's time is devoted to making money at the expense of "spending" time on other things (and people) that matter too, then no matter how much wealth one can accumulate, success will be a fleeting concept that will ultimately never satisfy.

Note what the writer of Proverbs says:
- Don't wear yourself out trying to get rich.
- Be wise enough to know when to quit.

Here is the reason why:
- In the blink of an eye wealth disappears, for it will sprout wings and fly away like an eagle.

A satisfied live will be yours as you TRUST GOD FOR WHAT YOU NEED and then allow Him, in His way, to PROVIDE ALL OF YOUR NEEDS.

Turn your POSITIVE DECLARATION OF QUALITY WISDOM into this prayer of commitment:

Lord Jesus, *Today May I* TRUST You FOR WHAT I NEED and then allow You, in Your way, to PROVIDE ALL OF MY NEEDS.

Keys To Experiencing Quality Wisdom For Life

What do you think is the key to trusting the Lord for meeting your needs, all of them?

Going Deeper In Bible Study

*I'll give you a few prompts in *bold type* to get you started. Then you can select one or two key words, phrases or doctrines in this passage of Scripture and follow the process by going through the three key elements of doing a meaningful Bible study (Observation, Interpretation, and Application):

Don't wear yourself out trying to get rich. Be wise enough to know when to quit.

In the blink of an eye wealth disappears, for it will sprout wings and fly away like an eagle. (Proverbs 23:4-5 NLT).

OBSERVATION: WHAT IS THE AUTHOR SAYING? {*key words, phrases or doctrines*}

INTERPRETATION: WHAT DOES IT MEAN? *{If you are doing a word study you may want to use a concordance. If you are studying a doctrine (a Biblical principle), can you give it a name? i.e., "the doctrine of . . . "}*

APPLICATION: HOW DOES IT APPLY TO ME? *{This is a key part of your Bible study. Read and pray through the Proverb again and review your thoughts on your notes on Observation and Interpretation then write out a concise personal application.}*

POSITIVE DECLARATION OF QUALITY WISDOM

Today May You . . . TRUST GOD FOR WHAT YOU NEED and then allow Him, in His way, to PROVIDE ALL OF YOUR NEEDS.

Don't wear yourself out trying to get rich. Be wise enough to know when to quit. In the blink of an eye wealth disappears, for it will sprout wings and fly away like an eagle. (Proverbs 23:4-5 NLT).

HOW THIS PROVERB CHALLENGES ME . . .

In my PERSONAL life

In my PROFESSIONAL life

In my SPIRITUAL life

DAY TWENTY-FOUR: "The Discerning Heart"

Today May You . . . give your heart to only those who will PROTECT it and not POISON it.

Don't envy evil people
or desire their company.
For their hearts plot violence,
and their words always stir up trouble. (Proverbs 24:1-2 NLT).

Quality Wisdom Devotional Thought:

Your heart is much too precious to expose it to those who will bring great harm to you. Protecting the heart is an intentional decision every day. God warns us about the dangers of putting our heart at risk, especially in the presence of those who are evil people.

Note the clear warning:

- Don't envy evil people—why envy anyone who does not have your core values?
- Don't desire their company—why would you want to be in the presence of someone who will leave a cloud of corruption over you?
- For their hearts plot violence—why link up with anyone who has a violent heart?
- Their words always stir up trouble—why be in the range of the sound of anyone's words who stir up trouble?

What is the best way to protect your heart? Give your heart to only those who will PROTECT it and not POISON it.

Turn your POSITIVE DECLARATION OF QUALITY WISDOM into this prayer of commitment:

Lord Jesus, *Today May I* give my heart to only those who will PROTECT it and not POISON it.

Keys To Experiencing Quality Wisdom For Life

What do you think is the key to protecting your heart from negative people?

Going Deeper In Bible Study

*I'll give you a few prompts in **bold type** to get you started. Then you can select one or two key words, phrases or doctrines in this passage of Scripture and follow the process by going through the three key elements of doing a meaningful Bible study (Observation, Interpretation, and Application):

Don't envy evil people

or desire their company.

For their hearts plot violence,

and their words always stir up trouble. (Proverbs 24:1-2 NLT).

OBSERVATION: WHAT IS THE AUTHOR SAYING? {*key words, phrases or doctrines*}

INTERPRETATION: WHAT DOES IT MEAN? *{If you are doing a word study you may want to use a concordance. If you are studying a doctrine (a Biblical principle), can you give it a name? i.e., "the doctrine of . . . "}*

APPLICATION: HOW DOES IT APPLY TO ME? *{This is a key part of your Bible study. Read and pray through the Proverb again and review your thoughts on your notes on Observation and Interpretation then write out a concise personal application.}*

POSITIVE DECLARATION OF QUALITY WISDOM

Today May You . . . give your heart to only those who will PROTECT it and not POISON it.

Don't envy evil people

or desire their company.

For their hearts plot violence,

and their words always stir up trouble. (Proverbs 24:1-2 NLT).

HOW THIS PROVERB CHALLENGES ME . . .

In my PERSONAL life

In my PROFESSIONAL life

In my SPIRITUAL life

DAY TWENTY-FIVE: "Promotion Comes From The Lord"

Today May You . . . allow the Lord to PROMOTE you before you PROMOTE yourself.

Don't demand an audience with the king

or push for a place among the great. It's better to wait for an invitation to the head table than to be sent away in public disgrace. (Proverbs 25:6-7 NLT).

Quality Wisdom Devotional Thought:

How to do you find the balance between pursuing your goals in your own strength and trusting the Lord to put you in the right place, at the right time, with the right opportunity, connected with the right person? It really comes down to TRUST. Do you trust the Lord to take care of you or is the internal pressure so great to take matters into your own hands and make something happen? The writer of Proverbs gives a clear distinction of the choices you make:

- Don't demand an audience with the king
- Don't push for a place among the great

In contrast:

- It's better to wait for an invitation to the head table than to be sent away in public disgrace.

This is true: God knows where you are, what you need, and when you need it. Knowing this, then **Today May You . . .** allow the Lord to PROMOTE you before you PROMOTE yourself.

Turn your **POSITIVE DECLARATION OF QUALITY WISDOM** into this prayer of commitment:

Lord Jesus, *Today May I* allow You to PROMOTE me before I PROMOTE myself.

Keys To Experiencing Quality Wisdom For Life

What do you think is the key in trusting the Lord to promote you, at the right time, in the right way?

Going Deeper In Bible Study

*I'll give you a few prompts in **bold type** to get you started. Then you can select one or two key words, phrases or doctrines in this passage of Scripture and follow the process by going through the three key elements of doing a meaningful Bible study (Observation, Interpretation, and Application):

Don't demand an audience with the king

or push for a place among the great. It's better to wait for an invitation to the head table than to be sent away in public disgrace. (Proverbs 25:6-7 NLT).

OBSERVATION: WHAT IS THE AUTHOR SAYING? {*key words, phrases or doctrines*}

INTERPRETATION: WHAT DOES IT MEAN? *{If you are doing a word study you may want to use a concordance. If you are studying a doctrine (a Biblical principle), can you give it a name? i.e., "the doctrine of . . . "}*

APPLICATION: HOW DOES IT APPLY TO ME? *{This is a key part of your Bible study. Read and pray through the Proverb again and review your thoughts on your notes on Observation and Interpretation then write out a concise personal application.}*

POSITIVE DECLARATION OF QUALITY WISDOM

Today May You . . . allow the Lord to PROMOTE you before you PROMOTE yourself.

Don't demand an audience with the king

or push for a place among the great. It's better to wait for an invitation to the head

table than to be sent away in public disgrace. (Proverbs 25:6-7 NLT).

HOW THIS PROVERB CHALLENGES ME . . .

In my PERSONAL life

In my PROFESSIONAL life

In my SPIRITUAL life

DAY TWENTY-SIX: "Spiritual Firefighter"

Today May You . . . resist the urge to join a gossip party and instead look for ways to speak well of those who are being slandered.

Fire goes out without wood,

and quarrels disappear when gossip stops. (Proverbs 26:20 NLT).

Quality Wisdom Devotional Thought:

The most powerful tool you have is your words. If they are crafted well, and intentionally targeted to another person's heart, your words can cause a massive infusion of life-giving encouragement. On the other hand, if you allow your words to become weaponized, they will become the cause of catastrophic destruction.

Living an intentional life that blesses others requires an intentional decision to carefully guard what comes out of our mouth knowing that fire goes out without wood, and quarrels disappear when gossip stops. So, resist the urge to join a gossip party and instead look for ways to speak well of those who are being slandered.

Turn your POSITIVE DECLARATION OF QUALITY WISDOM into this prayer of commitment:

Lord Jesus, *Today May I* resist the urge to join a gossip party and instead look for ways to speak well of those who are being slandered.

Keys To Experiencing Quality Wisdom For Life

What do you think is the key not to be a gossip?

Going Deeper In Bible Study

*I'll give you a few prompts in **bold type** to get you started. Then you can select one or two key words, phrases or doctrines in this passage of Scripture and follow the process by going through the three key elements of doing a meaningful Bible study (Observation, Interpretation, and Application):

Fire goes out without wood,
and quarrels disappear when gossip stops. (Proverbs 26:20 NLT).

OBSERVATION: WHAT IS THE AUTHOR SAYING? *{key words, phrases or*

doctrines}

INTERPRETATION: WHAT DOES IT MEAN? *{If you are doing a word study you may want to use a concordance. If you are studying a doctrine (a Biblical principle), can you give it a name? i.e., "the doctrine of . . . "}*

APPLICATION: HOW DOES IT APPLY TO ME? *{This is a key part of your Bible study. Read and pray through the Proverb again and review your thoughts on your notes on Observation and Interpretation then write out a concise personal application.}*

POSITIVE DECLARATION OF QUALITY WISDOM

Today May You . . . resist the urge to join a gossip party and instead look for ways to speak well of those who are being slandered.

Fire goes out without wood,

and quarrels disappear when gossip stops. (Proverbs 26:20 NLT).

HOW THIS PROVERB CHALLENGES ME . . .

In my PERSONAL life

In my PROFESSIONAL life

In my SPIRITUAL life

DAY TWENTY-SEVEN: "Present And Accounted For"

Today May You . . . live in the PRESENT and trust God to give you what you need for the FUTURE.

Don't brag about tomorrow,

since you don't know what the day will bring. (Proverbs 27:1 NLT).

Quality Wisdom Devotional Thought:

One of the most serious miscalculations we can make is to presume on what God's will (our future) will look like in the future. Every day people make predictions on financial investments, predictions how relationships will turn out, and even predictions on how long we will live. Only God knows. And we are not God and have no idea how the future will turn out, no matter what we think. Instead of predicting the future, we should be saying, "If the Lord wills . . . "

In no way is God saying to us to stop dreaming and not trust Him for His promises. But He does want us not to brag about tomorrow, since we don't know what the day will bring. So, today may you live in the PRESENT and trust God to give you what you need for the FUTURE.

Turn your POSITIVE DECLARATION OF QUALITY WISDOM into this prayer of commitment:

Lord Jesus, *Today May I* live in the PRESENT and trust God to give me what I need for the FUTURE.

Keys To Experiencing Quality Wisdom For Life

What do you think is the key to live in the present and not presume on what *may* happen in the future?

Going Deeper In Bible Study

*I'll give you a few prompts in **bold type** to get you started. Then you can select one or two key words, phrases or doctrines in this passage of Scripture and follow the process by going through the three key elements of doing a meaningful Bible study (Observation, Interpretation, and Application):

Don't brag about tomorrow,
since you don't know what the day will bring. (Proverbs 27:1 NLT).

OBSERVATION: WHAT IS THE AUTHOR SAYING? {*key words, phrases or doctrines*}

INTERPRETATION: WHAT DOES IT MEAN? {*If you are doing a word study you may want to use a concordance. If you are studying a doctrine (a Biblical principle), can you give it a name? i.e., "the doctrine of . . . "*}

APPLICATION: HOW DOES IT APPLY TO ME? {*This is a key part of your Bible study. Read and pray through the Proverb again and review your thoughts on your notes on Observation and Interpretation then write out a concise personal application.*}

POSITIVE DECLARATION OF QUALITY WISDOM

Today May You . . . live in the PRESENT and trust God to give you what you need for the FUTURE.

Don't brag about tomorrow,

since you don't know what the day will bring. (Proverbs 27:1 NLT).

HOW THIS PROVERB CHALLENGES ME . . .

In my PERSONAL life

In my PROFESSIONAL life

In my SPIRITUAL life

DAY TWENTY-EIGHT: "This Is My Country"

Today May You . . . pray for the kind of LEADERSHIP in your city, state, and country who would choose to be wise and knowledgeable and that the people would enjoy stability.

"When there is moral rot within a nation, its government topples easily. But wise and knowledgeable leaders bring stability." (Proverbs   28:2   NLT   ).

Quality Wisdom Devotional Thought:

Not everyone can be a political leader and all political leaders are not good leaders. But everyone can pray for our leaders. In the Old Testament, time and time again, the people were given leaders *they deserved!* The kings of Israel and Judah were only a reflection of the hearts of the people they led. We need to pray for our leaders, and we need to pray for ourselves too. Why? Because of the incredible benefits that come our way when we do pray for our leaders:

'I urge you, first of all, to pray for all people. Ask God to help them; intercede on their behalf, and give thanks for them. Pray this way for kings and all who are in authority so that we can live peaceful and quiet lives marked by godliness and dignity. '(1 Timothy 2:1-2 NLT).

So, if there is moral rot in your nation, your government is at risk for catastrophic failure. But if the Lord blesses your nation with wise and knowledgeable leaders your nation will experience stability. The challenge for you is to pray for the kind of LEADERSHIP in your city, state, and country who would choose to be wise and knowledgeable and that the people would enjoy stability.

Turn your POSITIVE DECLARATION OF QUALITY WISDOM into this prayer of commitment:

Lord Jesus, *Today May I* pray for the kind of LEADERSHIP in my city, state, and country who would choose to be wise and knowledgeable and that the people would enjoy stability.

Keys To Experiencing Quality Wisdom For Life

What do you think is the key to adding salt and light to your community?

Going Deeper In Bible Study

*I'll give you a few prompts in *bold type* to get you started. Then you can select one or two key words, phrases or doctrines in this passage of Scripture and follow the process by going through the three key elements of doing a meaningful Bible study (Observation, Interpretation, and Application):

"When there is moral rot within a nation, its government topples easily. But wise and knowledgeable leaders bring stability." (Proverbs   28:2   NLT   ).

OBSERVATION: WHAT IS THE AUTHOR SAYING? {*key words, phrases or doctrines*}

INTERPRETATION: WHAT DOES IT MEAN? *{If you are doing a word study you may want to use a concordance. If you are studying a doctrine (a Biblical principle), can you give it a name? i.e., "the doctrine of . . . "}*

APPLICATION: HOW DOES IT APPLY TO ME? *{This is a key part of your Bible study. Read and pray through the Proverb again and review your thoughts on your notes on Observation and Interpretation then write out a concise personal application.}*

POSITIVE DECLARATION OF QUALITY WISDOM

Today May You . . . pray for the kind of LEADERSHIP in your city, state, and country who would choose to be wise and knowledgeable and that the people would enjoy stability.

"When there is moral rot within a nation, its government topples easily. But wise and knowledgeable leaders bring stability." (Proverbs   28:2   NLT   ).

HOW THIS PROVERB CHALLENGES ME . . .

In my PERSONAL life

In my PROFESSIONAL life

In my SPIRITUAL life

DAY TWENTY-NINE: "A Big Heart Is A Caring Heart"

Today May You . . . have a BIG heart for the people who need your COMPASSION and your CARE.

The godly care about the rights of the poor;

the wicked don't care at all. (Proverbs 29:7 NLT).

Quality Wisdom Devotional Thought:

What does it cost to care? It depends. Does it cost you your time? Or does it cost you your material resources? Or is it both? Counting the cost always requires a decision. And how you come to that decision is a pretty reliable indicator of who are and what you value. In this Proverb, there are two value statements:

- The godly care about the rights of the poor
- The wicked don't care at all

Right is right and rights are the rights for everyone, including the ones who are most at risk in the hands of powerful people, the poor. One of the most noble (and Christ-like) acts you can do is to be godly and then care about the rights of the poor. It is the callus person, the ungodly person who has a heart of stone and does not care at all.

If you really want to make a difference, then have a BIG heart for the people who need your COMPASSION and your CARE.

Turn your POSITIVE DECLARATION OF QUALITY WISDOM into this prayer of commitment:

Lord Jesus, *Today May I* have a BIG heart for the people who need my COMPASSION and my CARE.

Keys To Experiencing Quality Wisdom For Life

What do you think is the key to adding value to the least of these?

Going Deeper In Bible Study

*I'll give you a few prompts in **bold type** to get you started. Then you can select one or two key words, phrases or doctrines in this passage of Scripture and follow the process by going through the three key elements of doing a meaningful Bible study (Observation, Interpretation, and Application):

The godly care about the rights of the poor;

the wicked don't care at all. (Proverbs 29:7 NLT).

OBSERVATION: WHAT IS THE AUTHOR SAYING? {*key words, phrases or doctrines*}

INTERPRETATION: WHAT DOES IT MEAN? *{If you are doing a word study you may want to use a concordance. If you are studying a doctrine (a Biblical principle), can you give it a name? i.e., "the doctrine of . . . "}*

APPLICATION: HOW DOES IT APPLY TO ME? *{This is a key part of your Bible study. Read and pray through the Proverb again and review your thoughts on your notes on Observation and Interpretation then write out a concise personal application.}*

POSITIVE DECLARATION OF QUALITY WISDOM

Today May You . . . have a BIG heart for the people who need your COMPASSION and your CARE.

The godly care about the rights of the poor;

the wicked don't care at all. (Proverbs 29:7 NLT).

HOW THIS PROVERB CHALLENGES ME . . .

In my PERSONAL life

In my PROFESSIONAL life

In my SPIRITUAL life

DAY THIRTY: "The Blessing Of Giving Your Big Problems To A Bigger God"

Today May You . . . give your big problems to a BIGGER God.

Who but God goes up to heaven and comes back down?

Who holds the wind in his fists?

Who wraps up the oceans in his cloak?

Who has created the whole wide world?

What is his name—and his son's name?

Tell me if you know! (Proverbs 30:4 NLT).

Quality Wisdom Devotional Thought:

"That's impossible!!!" Ever let those words escape from your mouth when you've come to the end of your rope and the only option left is a miracle? Fortunately, for the believer, that is always the best option. Big problems need to be submitted to a bigger God. If your big problems are bigger than your God, then you become the solution to your problems. Good luck with that!

Let's dissect this Proverb, line by line, by asking the question, answering it, and then make a life application.

- Who but God goes up to heaven and comes back down? No one but God.
- Who holds the wind in his fists? No one but God.
- Who wraps up the oceans in his cloak? No one but God.
- Who has created the whole wide world? No one but God.
- What is his name—and his son's name? He is the Lord God Almighty and His Son's name is Jesus.

When you can take the focus OFF of your problems and put your focus ON God then you will experience the blessing of giving your problems to a bigger God.

Turn your POSITIVE DECLARATION OF QUALITY WISDOM into this prayer of commitment:

Lord Jesus, *Today May I* give my big problems to a BIGGER God.

Keys To Experiencing Quality Wisdom For Life:

What do you think is the key to keeping your obstacles with the right perspective?

Going Deeper In Bible Study

*I'll give you a few prompts in *bold type* to get you started. Then you can select one or two key words, phrases or doctrines in this passage of Scripture and follow the process by going through the three key elements of doing a meaningful Bible study (Observation, Interpretation, and Application):

Who but God goes up to heaven and comes back down?

Who holds the wind in his fists?

Who wraps up the oceans in his cloak?

Who has created the whole wide world?

What is his name—and his son's name?

Tell me if you know! (Proverbs 30:4 NLT).

OBSERVATION: WHAT IS THE AUTHOR SAYING? {*key words, phrases or doctrines*}

INTERPRETATION: WHAT DOES IT MEAN? *{If you are doing a word study you may want to use a concordance. If you are studying a doctrine (a Biblical principle), can you give it a name? i.e., "the doctrine of . . . "}*

APPLICATION: HOW DOES IT APPLY TO ME? *{This is a key part of your Bible study. Read and pray through the Proverb again and review your thoughts on your notes on Observation and Interpretation then write out a concise personal application.}*

POSITIVE DECLARATION OF QUALITY WISDOM

Today May You . . . give your big problems to a BIGGER God.

Who but God goes up to heaven and comes back down?

Who holds the wind in his fists?

Who wraps up the oceans in his cloak?

Who has created the whole wide world?

What is his name—and his son's name?

Tell me if you know! (Proverbs 30:4 NLT).

HOW THIS PROVERB CHALLENGES ME . . .

In my PERSONAL life

In my PROFESSIONAL life

In my SPIRITUAL life

DAY THIRTY-ONE: "The Power And Responsibility Of Being An Advocate"

Today May You . . . use your INFLUENCE to INTERCEDE for those who are INNOCENT.

Speak up for those who cannot speak for themselves;

ensure justice for those being crushed.

Yes, speak up for the poor and helpless,

and see that they get justice. (Proverbs 31:8-9 NLT).

Quality Wisdom Devotional Thought:

One of the greatest and most precious gifts that God can give a person is the gift of power. It's when a leader is trusted with power and influence the heart is revealed. Power is a stewardship issue and how it is used defines a person's effectiveness in either blessing those who are at a power disadvantage or overlooking them. This Proverb is filled with intentional choices that matter:

- Speak up for those who cannot speak for themselves: This requires an intentional action.

- Ensure justice for those being crushed: This requires an intentional action.

- Yes, speak up for the poor and helpless: This requires an intentional action.

- And see that they get justice: This requires an intentional action.

If you are serious about using your position of power, then use your INFLUENCE to INTERCEDE for those who are INNOCENT.

Turn your POSITIVE DECLARATION OF QUALITY WISDOM into this prayer of commitment:

Lord Jesus, *Today May I* use my INFLUENCE to INTERCEDE for those who are INNOCENT.

Keys To Experiencing Quality Wisdom For Life

What do you think is the key to becoming an effective advocate for those who need an advocate?

Going Deeper In Bible Study

*I'll give you a few prompts in **bold type** to get you started. Then you can select one or two key words, phrases or doctrines in this passage of Scripture and follow the process by going through the three key elements of doing a meaningful Bible study (Observation, Interpretation, and Application):

Speak up for those who cannot speak for themselves;

ensure justice for those being crushed.

Yes, speak up for the poor and helpless,

and see that they get justice. (Proverbs 31:8-9 NLT).

OBSERVATION: WHAT IS THE AUTHOR SAYING? {*key words, phrases or doctrines*}

INTERPRETATION: WHAT DOES IT MEAN? *{If you are doing a word study you may want to use a concordance. If you are studying a doctrine (a Biblical principle), can you give it a name? i.e., "the doctrine of . . . "}*

APPLICATION: HOW DOES IT APPLY TO ME? *{This is a key part of your Bible study. Read and pray through the Proverb again and review your thoughts on your notes on Observation and Interpretation then write out a concise personal application.}*

POSITIVE DECLARATION OF QUALITY WISDOM

Today May You . . . use your INFLUENCE to INTERCEDE for those who are INNOCENT.

Speak up for those who cannot speak for themselves;

ensure justice for those being crushed.

Yes, speak up for the poor and helpless,

and see that they get justice. (Proverbs 31:8-9 NLT).

HOW THIS PROVERB CHALLENGES ME . . .

In my PERSONAL life

In my PROFESSIONAL life

In my SPIRITUAL life

Summary: 31 Prayers Of Commitment / Action Points

Exercise: Set aside a block of time where you can pray, uninterrupted, these 31 prayers. Don't just "read" through them. Instead, pray, ponder, and reflect upon each one. To make it even more profound, pray these prayers outloud. Allow the intimate presence of the Lord flow over your heart as you pray.

Lord Jesus, *Today May I* have a heart that is open to wisdom, a mind that is willing to be disciplined, and have an unswerving commitment to do what is right, just, and fair.

Lord Jesus, *Today May I* place a HIGH VALUE on the Lord's wisdom and the grace He gives for me to understand what to do with His wisdom.

Lord Jesus, *Today May I* TRUST You with everything I've got instead of TRUSTING me with everything I have, and as I live my life, I will TRUST Your will to take me where I need to go.

Lord Jesus, *Today May I* GET WISDOM before foolishness gets me.

Lord Jesus, *Today May I* LOOK UP before I LOOK DOWN so that I may STAY OUT OF TROUBLE.

Lord Jesus, *Today May I* embrace the life teachings from my spiritual parents (Mentors) and live a life marked by success.

Lord Jesus, *Today May I* do whatever it takes to keep my eyes on the PRIZE of experiencing the abundant life and keep myself from stumbling into the PIT of despair.

Lord Jesus, *Today May I* cling to every bit of wisdom I can collect . . . and use it.

Lord Jesus, *Today May I* make an intentional investment in people who are serious about becoming an even better version of themselves.

Lord Jesus, *Today May I* make it my goal not to be a "Christian" businessman or businesswoman but to be a businessman or businesswoman who TRUSTS God, who LIVES for God, who LOVES like God, and who is BLESSED by God.

Lord Jesus, *Today May I* make sure my moral compass is true in every business and personal relationship transaction I make.

Lord Jesus, *Today May I* LOVE humility so that I may embrace discipline and correction and LEARN.
Lord Jesus, *Today May I* watch what I say so I will not have to eat my words.

Lord Jesus, *Today May I* make decisions that keep me on the RIGHT path, connecting me with the RIGHT people, and help me wind up in the RIGHT place.

Lord Jesus, *Today May I* WATCH what I say, WHO I say it to, and HOW I say it.

Lord Jesus, *Today May I* be free to dream a dream that only God can fulfill.

Lord Jesus, *Today May I* keep my integrity in what I think and in what I say and in what I do.

Lord Jesus, *Today May I* be a plentiful resource of wisdom that wisdom hunters can come and draw from me.

Lord Jesus, *Today May I* be HONEST with others, HONEST with myself, and HONEST to God.

Lord Jesus, *Today May I* take the HIGH road and walk over those who are UNDER the road.

Lord Jesus, *Today May I* check my HEART before I trust my EYES.

Lord Jesus, *Today May I* live like CHARACTER matters more than my material COMFORT.

Lord Jesus, *Today May I* TRUST You FOR WHAT I NEED and then allow You, in Your way, to PROVIDE ALL OF MY NEEDS.

Lord Jesus, *Today May I* give my heart to only those who will PROTECT it and not POISON it.

Lord Jesus, *Today May I* allow You to PROMOTE me before I PROMOTE myself.

Lord Jesus, *Today May I* resist the urge to join a gossip party and instead look for ways to speak well of those who are being slandered.

Lord Jesus, *Today May I* live in the PRESENT and trust God to give me what I need for the FUTURE.

Lord Jesus, *Today May I* pray for the kind of LEADERSHIP in my city, state, and country who would choose to be wise and knowledgeable and that the people would enjoy stability.

Lord Jesus, *Today May I* have a BIG heart for the people who need my COMPASSION and my CARE.

Lord Jesus, *Today May I* give my big problems to a BIGGER God.

Lord Jesus, *Today May I* use my INFLUENCE to INTERCEDE for those who are INNOCENT.

HOW YOU CAN HAVE
A RELATIONSHIP WITH JESUS

✓ GOD LOVES YOU AND HAS A WONDERFUL PLAN FOR YOUR LIFE

For I know the plans I have for you," declares the LORD, "plans to prosper you and not to harm you, plans to give you hope and a future. **Jeremiah 29:11 (NIV)**

✓ AS A RESULT OF MAN GOING HIS OWN WAY AND REJECTING GOD, A CHASM, A GREAT DIVIDE, HAS COME SEPARATING A JUST AND HOLY GOD FROM SINFUL MAN

for all have sinned and fall short of the glory of God, **Romans 3:23 (NIV)**

For the wages of sin is death, but the gift of God is eternal life in Christ Jesus our Lord. **Romans 6:23 (NIV)**

✓ GOD SENT HIS SON, HIS PERFECT SON TO BECOME OUR SACRIFICE. HE WHO IS SINLESS TOOK UPON HIMSELF OUR SINS, OFFERING TO RESTORE OUR BROKEN RELATIONSHIP WITH GOD, BRIDGING THE GAP BETWEEN GOD AND MAN

We all, like sheep, have gone astray, each of us has turned to his own way; and the LORD has laid on him the iniquity of us all. **Isaiah 53:6 (NIV)**

The next day John saw Jesus coming toward him and said, "Look, the Lamb of God, who takes away the sin of the world!" **John 1:29 (NIV)**

✓ GOD HAS GIVEN EACH MAN A CHOICE EITHER TO ACCEPT THE FREE GIFT OF SALVATION AND LIVE FOREVER OR TO REJECT HIS GRACIOUS GIFT AND SPEND ETERNITY FOREVER SEPARATED FROM GOD

For God so loved the world that he gave his one and only Son, that whoever believes in him shall not perish but have eternal life. **John 3:16 (NIV)**

[12]Yet to all who received him, to those who believed in his name, he gave the right to become children of God-- [13]children born not of natural descent, nor of human decision or a husband's will, but born of God. **John 1:12-13 (NIV)**

Essential Spiritual Growth Resources from Something New Christian Publishers and Quality Leadership Consultants

Websites, Newsletter, and Blogs:

www.dennybates.com and www.ReallyGoodDay4U.com is the hub for all of our teaching and coaching resources. Check out our free downloads as well as our store.

www.thequalitydisciple.com links to dennybates.com.

www.qualityleadershipconsultants.com links to dennybates.com.

www.thequalitydisciple.blogspot.com is the teaching blog for Psalms of Discipleship.

www.facebook.com/denny.bates is my portal to social networking.

Dr. Denny Bates and Quality Leadership Tips For You is my newsletter. Featured leadership articles, devotional thoughts, and a menu of coaching and book resources.

Sign up at http://www.dennybates.com You can follow me on Twitter @dennybates

Books:
Other titles from the Quality Discipleship Series:
- ❖ How To Study And Apply The Bible To Your Life (PDF Book only)
- ❖ Growing Up…Practical Bible Studies For New And Growing Christians (PDF Book only)
- ❖ Psalms of Discipleship: A One Year Journey With The Shepherd (Kindle or printed copy)
- ❖ Christmas Meditations of Worship: Four Weeks of Advent (Kindle or printed copy)
- ❖ Living Above The Fray: Learning The Seven Healthy Leadership Principles That Will Shelter You From The Destructive Effects Of Leader-I-Tis (Kindle or printed copy)
- ❖ My Spiritual Life Plan: Creating An Effective Spiritual Life Plan For The Quality Disciple (Kindle or printed copy)
- ❖ Living Above The Fray Leadership Assessment: The Coaches Guide For Leading With Quality In Mind (Kindle or printed copy)
- ❖ Building A Christian Community Of Friends: Four Practical Studies On Biblical Friendships (Kindle or printed copy)
- ❖ Changing Places: Understanding The Process Of Transition. (Kindle or printed copy)
- ❖ Life-Ol-Ogy: Mastering The Study Of Your Life, Your Team, Your Profession and Your Customers (Kindle or printed copy)
- ❖ Growing In Greatness: *31 Living Legacy Principles From the Proverbs For the Quality Leader (Proverbs 1:1-5:14), Volume 1* (Kindle or printed copy)

- ❖ Quality Wisdom For A Modern Age: The Wisdom Book Of Proverbs (Kindle or printed copy)
- ❖ Coming in 2020!!! Living Beyond The Fray: *How Bitter Busters Can Set You Free From Becoming Bitter Against Family, Friends, Career, Church and God."*

Retreat Journals:
- ❖ The Power – Broker's Guide To The Kingdom
- ❖ Four Legacies For A Life Change
- ❖ Three Commitments That Change A Life
- ❖ Growing In Grace: A Fresh Look At Biblical Discipleship
- ❖ Adding Quality To Your Life

Help Me Write My Story Books (A ghost writing and book coaching custom service)

For information see next page or connect to **www.HelpMeWriteMyStory.com**.

- ❖ "Touched by Him: A Man Who Said Yes To Jesus" by Harry F. Lyles as told
  to Dr. Denny Bates (Unpublished)
- ❖ "I'm Just Rebeckah Wilhelmina And I Found A Way Out" by Rebeckah Wilhelmina (Healthy Curves Count Publishers)
- ❖ "The Blue Duck: Learning How To Discover Your Competitive Edge And Celebrate The Uniqueness Of You" by Sandra Mason (Younique Publishers)
- ❖ "How To Kick Your Own Butt: The Fine Art Of Leading Yourself Well" by Carol Mabe (CMC Transformational Publishing)
- ❖ "My Life: Then And Now: Won't He Do It" by Karen Calhoun (KMJC Publishers)
- ❖ "Take the Soap" by Bryan Braddock, Byon "kNOw Ca$h" McCullough as told to Dr. Denny Bates (Take The Soap Publishers—Coming in 2020)

Contact us for availability and cost.
www.dennybates.com

What is your story?

Help Me Write My Story (HMWMS)
www.HelpMeWriteMyStory.com

HELP ME WRITE MY STORY is a highly relational, process-driven, professional service that empowers an aspiring author to produce a personal memoir that is shared in a self-published book (including Kindle too). HELP ME WRITE MY STORY helps you to focus on this acrostic:

H = **Heartfelt** (The best place to begin writing your story is in the HEART)

M = **Memories** (If you do not WRITE THEM DOWN you will eventually FORGET many of them)

W = **Well-spoken** (To tell your story you've got to be a CLEAR COMMUNICATOR so you will be understood)

M = **Motivational** (It's important for you not to only share with your readers how CHALLENGING your circumstances may have been but it's even more important to share how you faced your obstacles and got through them SUCCESSFULLY)

S = **Strategic** (Your story will most likely not speak to everyone, but it will speak to SOMEONE, so it's important to know WHO you are seeking to influence the most and why)

I believe that our lives are the sum of many stories filled with adventures, wonders, disappointments, successes, tragedies, victories, and mysteries. Our **STORIES**, all of them, have the necessary components for a lasting legacy.

Your story is a **GIFT** to others. Your life is a **STEWARDSHIP**. Your story matters because **YOU MATTER**. Your story needs to be **SHARED** with and **REMEMBERED** by those who need to KNOW your story.

That said, many **STORIES** never go beyond the back of our minds and fade away forever. And that is why I am writing to you. I want to help you **WRITE YOUR STORY**.

IMAGINE for a moment what you could do with **YOUR STORY** in the **FORM** of a **BOOK**:

- **YOUR STORY**, in the form of a quality published book, becomes something tangible and is in your hands.

- **YOUR STORY** can give encouragement to others, especially to your family, friends, and customers/clients, and even to people you will unlikely ever meet in this life.

- **YOUR STORY** contains your legacy and will always be there, even after you are long gone, influencing future readers.

- **YOUR STORY**, in the form of a book, will be the perfect and unique item for you to give away or sell, creating a new revenue stream.

- **YOUR STORY** can serve as a mentor to help the person who wants to learn how to apply the life lessons you experienced.

YOUR STORY matters to you and **YOUR STORY** matters to me too.

What is HELP ME WRITE MY STORY?

HELP ME WRITE MY STORY coaches the author client through each creative phase of writing a book:

- How to create the Big Story Idea

- How to create a *Write My Story Time Line*

- How to do great research

- How to create a strong outline of chapters and subchapters

- How to use creative words to paint vivid mental and emotional images

- How to tell your story in an interesting way

- How to write strong chapter summaries

- How to create of book title and subtitle that resonates with the reader

- How to create a book front and back cover that catches the reader's attention

- How to write back cover copy

- How to take an author's story to the finished product in print and in Kindle formats.

- How to use the power of social networking to promote your story

Who needs HELP ME WRITE MY STORY?

HELP ME WRITE MY STORY can be a great resource for the person who . . .

- Wants to write their story but need practical instruction, intentional coaching and accountability.

- Wants to make sure their story, their legacy, is preserved in a format so family members and friends will remember and be inspired by their story.

- Wants to use their story as a way to open doors of future opportunities for even greater influence.

- Wants a personal product to either sell or gift to others.

- Wants the rewarding satisfaction of having a professional copy of their personal story.

How does HELP ME WRITE MY STORY work?

Each writing project has its own unique set of challenges, but I've sought to present three different packages and pricing levels. All five are dependent upon the pace, progress, and extraordinary challenges of the book.

There are five Story Coaching service levels of Help Me Write My Story*:

In addition to the fees for each package, a reduced monthly payment plus a percentage of the royalties is an alternative form of payment. See me for the details.

Help Me Write My Story Books is a ghost writing and book coaching custom service. For information connect to **www.HelpMeWriteMyStory.com**

QUALITY LEADERSHIP CONSULTANTS

PROFESSIONAL COACHING, CONSULTING,
AND TEACHING
Presenting Quality Ideas;
Producing Quality Leaders

Introducing Dr. Denny Bates
Professional Life, Business Coach, Teacher, Writer, Speaker And Consultant

DR. DENNY BATES
LEADING WITH QUALITY IN MIND

Why is it important for you to have a professional quality life coach and leadership trainer?

It has been said, "Experience is the best guide in life." The truth is *guided experience* is the best guide! Time, money, and emotional energy can be saved by linking up with a person who already understands where you are, where you want to go and has a good grasp on how to lead you there in a positive way.

What kind of guided
experience do I offer?

Seasoned in both the market place and non-profit settings, I can offer you and/or your organization Quality Leadership coaching tracks with a relational emphasis. For instance: Personal Growth, Communication Skills, Building Healthy Relationships, Career Counseling / Job Performance, Life Transitions, Organizational Health; and for faith-based individuals and/or organizations, Spiritual Growth. My practical experience in both for-profit and non-profit settings, coupled with my academic and professional training, affords me the ability to offer you unique Quality Leadership services.

The JOHN MAXWELL **Team**

AN INDEPENDENT CERTIFIED COACH, TEACHER AND SPEAKER
WITH THE JOHN MAXWELL TEAM

My friend John Maxwell says,

"Everything rises and falls on leadership"

As a Leadership Specialist,
I can help YOU in the marketplace!

✓ With years of experience working as a manager in the marketplace, I know what it takes to create a healthy organization. I can train your leaders and employees in effective teamwork and communication.

✓ I know how to help business leaders practice the kind of self-care that not only benefits them personally, but also adds value to the company.

✓ I know how to help a management team build a culture that places great value on integrity and success.

✓ I can help you and your leaders set reasonable goals and show you the tools to help you reach each one.

✓ I can help you reproduce your values, vision and passion in the lives of others.

✓ I can help you sharpen your leadership skills in a group coaching setting or one to one. As a professional life coach and leadership trainer, I can offer you the finest coaching and training resources available today as a certified coach, teacher and speaker for the John Maxwell Team.

QUALITY
LEADERSHIP CONSULTANTS
Email dennybates@gmail.com
www.dennybates.com

What does a Disciple-Making Ministry look like?
It looks like . . .

SOMETHING *new*

"Do not call to mind the former things, or ponder things of the past; Behold, I will do something new . . ."
Isaiah 43:18, 19a

- Is a ministry that focuses upon making Quality disciples for Jesus

- Is a ministry that encourages believers to connect in community and experience the discipled life

- Is a ministry that seeks to help other body of believers to learn how to live the discipled life through seminars, workshops, keynote speaking and interactive coaching

Contact Dr. Denny Bates for more information on how you and your church can create a culture of DiscipleMakers4Jesus

www.TheQualityDisciple.com

What Others Are Saying About My Leadership Coaching And Discipleship Via DiscipleMakers4Jesus (DM4J)

I know and have worked with Denny Bates for more than a decade. Denny now serves as a leadership trainer and coach. It is my pleasure to recommend Denny as a valuable and trusted resource for leadership training and coaching. In addition to earning his doctoral degree in leadership, Denny is also an independent certified coach, teacher, and speaker for The John Maxwell Team. I believe you and your organization will benefit from his knowledge of what leaders need in order to grow as a leader. You will appreciate Denny's relational approach to leadership training and his ability to connect with people. Dr. Bates offers workshops, seminars, keynote speaking, and coaching ... aiding your personal and professional growth through study and practical application of John Maxwell's leadership methods. **(President and CEO of Regional Hospital)**

Just wanted to let you know how much our time of coaching and leadership development has meant to me. Every time I am faced with a challenge I try to walk thru the Grace tree of wisdom. You set the example every day of the man of God I want to be. Thank you! **(Corporate Manager of Medical Services)**

[I've learned] to keep the main thing the main thing!! To take care of the people that God puts in front of me everyday. **(Sales Manager of automotive dealership)**

Denny has been my friend, pastor, colleague, mentor and confidant for almost 10 years. During this time, Denny has led me through tough waters, given me wise counsel and taught me practical ways to live out my faith while falling more in love with my Savior. **(Youth Pastor)**

Other than my own father, Denny has been my most trusted friend and spiritual mentor. Denny's discipleship has been truly transforming and helped me to realize the importance of investing in others as he has invested in me. **(Medical Device Consultant)**

I treasure my relationship with Denny because we share a common heart to help people discover all that Christ wants to do in and through them. **(Disciple-Making Missionary to Eastern Europe)**

I have known Denny for many years and have had the privilege to work with him on the same pastoral staff for over 5 years. During that time I have sought Denny's counsel on many issues ranging from personal struggles to theological questions. Denny has always provided me with poignant, gracious and thoughtful counsel. They say that everyone should have a mentor and I am blessed to be able to consider Denny my mentor. He has been an invaluable asset in my life and ministry. **(Clinical Counselor)**

My relationship with Denny has been personal, honest, and Christ-centered. Denny's common sense approach to the issues of life is always soundly based on scriptural principles. I remember discussing with Denny how I felt that I needed to do so much service for the Lord because of all the times I had failed Him. Denny gently said to me, "It's all about grace". I was reminded that there is no 'payback' plan for the Lord. *(Pastor)*

Having a group of peers who candidly discuss the awesome responsibility that each carries as a servant and hearing how God has responded so richly to our needs clearly demonstrates how marvelous is our God, who works in each of our lives to do His will. *(Hospital Vice-President in a discipleship group for executives)*

Denny and I have know each other for nearly fifteen years, we bonded shortly after he had his heart attack because of an illness I had years prior — Guillain-Barre Syndrome — that made me more aware of the right priorities I should have in life. Through this episode and having children similar in age we bonded in a unique and special way rarely achieved between men. Approximately one year ago I lost my job as a senior executive at a large international company that I had been with 26 years, during the transition period of me finding another job Denny was an extreme encouragement to me. During a time when I was wrestling between accepting a position or not and I will never forget what Denny told me "You can just accept it as God's providential care". He was right! I later humbly accepted the position as President & Chief Operating Officer for a Subsea Oilfield Manufacturing company. *(Corporate Executive)*

Denny has been a teacher / mentor / discipler / encourager / prayer partner and great friend who God has used to help me keep a godly perspective on the different times & issues of life I've gone through as I've seek to follow Jesus. Once while praying with Denny through a career move, he encouraged me to think of the gifts & skills I had and then ask what I had a passion for, and then to ask God to show me how they can fit together. From this I learned to stop putting these gifts & skills in a "Box" and limiting what God could do with them, and use them for. For the first time, as I now work for a non-profit Christian organization as a warehouse manager, I feel I'm using the gifts and abilities God has given me to fulfill His purpose at something I really have a passion for! *(Former market place worker, now Missionary who is impacting the world)*

Denny met with me at 7 a.m. every Friday for a year. He came to me knowing he would receive my weekly burdens. This is not the way any of us would choose to begin our day. He does not judge nor do I ever feel judged. He is one of the most selfless and giving person I have ever met. This is easy to say because I know he is just a man. His obedience to God sets him apart. He taught me to live by grace, be long suffering, and love my wife regardless of my excuses. *(Medical Worker, Physical therapist assistant)*

Through a lifestyle of disciple making, Denny Bates has shown me what it truly means to live out

Matthew 28: 19, 20. **(*Educator*)**

I've heard it said that on this side of eternity that there are only two things that you can be certain of: death and taxes. I'm certain of three things; the first two and that I have a friend in Denny Bates! I asked God at the beginning of my ministry to bring solid men into my life that would disciple me, teach me and hold me accountable. Denny has been an extreme answer to that prayer. **(*Church-planting Pastor*)**

Dr. Denny Bates opened my eyes to the power of small groups. He showed me what a true mentor really is. I will be forever grateful for his leadership, friendship, and love! **(*Videographer*)**

Practical application of God's teachings by normal, everyday family men such as myself; that's what DM4J means to me. Listening to and sharing the innumerable ways the Lord touches the lives of each and every man in this group is not only uplifting, but inspiring. From the greatest trials to what might seem trivial, God has a plan and a purpose for it all. The value of DM4J to me is immeasurable. **(*Pharmacist*)**

Praise For Quality Wisdom For A Modern Age:

For me, reading from the book of Proverbs has always felt a bit like trying to drink water from a fire hydrant - too much comes at me at one time and it overwhelms me. In *Quality Living For a Modern Age*, Dr. Denny Bates has meticulously broken down this powerful, timeless Old Testament book of wise instruction into day by day "bite size" truths enabling the reader to apply each truth and get the very most out of the Scriptures. The *Prayer of Commitment* found at the end of each devotion is guaranteed to help the reader in their personal growth. This is one book you will not want to hurry through. It's great for family devotions as well.
~ Kirby King, inspirational speaker and Bible teacher; author of *Abiding in Christ: What Is it Anyway?* and *Walking Through Fire Without Getting Burned: Finding Hope In The Hard Places*

Dr. Denny Bates has a fabulous unique way to share his wealth of quality wisdom with his readers. The devotions will lift, stretch, encourage, and press you forward. Your strongest challenge may very well be the fact that you don't want to part ways and lay the book down. Just as there is a Proverbs chapter for every day of the month, this devotional will provide you with what I like to call the icing on the cake. As you begin your journey you will want to keep this book close by at all times!
~ Carol Mabe, Life Coach, Leadership Trainer, Speaker, Author of *Kick Your Own Butt: The Fine Art Of Leading Yourself Well*

Denny Bates's *Quality Wisdom for A Modern Age* is valuable for two reasons. One, it lays our Christian principles that professionals can immediately apply to their career. Two, it is an ongoing resource of daily encouragement that can be used by new and seasoned Christians alike.
~ Traci McCombs, Author and Blogger

What a wonderful daily encouragement! Dr. Denny Bates has dissected the book of Proverbs to highlight the wisdom God has provided for us in this great book of the Bible. I believe this daily devotional will help you apply Proverbs' eternal truths in a more practical and relevant way that will assist you in your everyday Christian walk. I highly recommend *Quality Wisdom for a Modern Age* for your daily study of God's Word.
~ Ron Lyles
Owner, Schofield's Hardware and Sporting Goods
Board Trustee, Leadership Ministries Worldwide

The book of Proverbs is a phenomenal book. It is such an inspiration on what, where, who God is. It helps in our daily walk. It gives you strength, wisdom, discernment for life. It gives practical ways to look at life through God's lenses. I would highly recommend *Quality Wisdom for a Modern Age*.
~ Cleo Corey, author and life coach

Denny inspires me. His thoughts captured in this book will warm your heart and challenge your mind. Get ready to consume fresh words of wisdom.
~ Kary Oberbrunner, author of *Your Secret Name, the Deeper Path, and Day Job to Dream Job*

I love the book of Proverbs. I love how you quote and simplify the meaning of each verse to give an easy understanding of this great book. Any person who reads your book will be helped by being able to apply scripture to reality. Absolutely incredible book Denny. God bless you.
~ Traceyann Pearl Brough, author of *Heaven's Got A Plan For You*

You will find that as you read this book your thoughts are transformed, and your emotions are empowered with life. God will meet you in it as you take the journey from one page into the next. I highly recommend because it is engaging, and you will gain insight to your daily life in an enjoyable way. He has presented challenges that are relatable with answers that are attainable.
~ Laura Harris, Artist, Design Director at No Other Wall

Proverbs is my favorite book in the Bible. Primarily because of its consistent message regarding wisdom. As a Christian business leader, I am responsible for leading my team and truly making a positive difference. I never want to come up short. God enables us with unique gifts/talents, but he holds us responsible to develop those talents; this book is a great place to start. I've known Denny for some time, and he has always been passionate about Christian leadership and helping those leaders do their very best in garnering the necessary wisdom to lead well.
~ Rick Saunders
President/CEO, First Reliance Bank

I remember the day I first met Denny Bates. It was his welcoming smile that made me think of Jesus. His humor and warmth put me at ease. I knew this would be someone I would collaborate with, share advice with, and enjoy as a longtime friend. With this new published work of his, *Quality Wisdom For A Modern Age*, I can see how Denny truly fathers others in the faith. He is a disciple-maker and this new book, and its easy-to-read format will help shape the next generation of believers.
~ Robin L. Lewis,
Author of *The Guts and Glory Of Forgiveness: Living Healed*, speaker, and Christ-centered life coach

I am a very simple thinker…I really enjoyed the 31 days….simple and short…to the point….easy for me to follow.
~ Wick Jackson
Envoy International, Director

In the short time I've known Denny, I have come to find him as a very dedicated man of God, who chooses daily to walk the high road, while encouraging everyone he meets to join him. Denny doesn't just offer you a kind word and send you on your way, but rather, he demonstrates a genuine interest in and concern for others ability to maneuver through the stuff of life and come out better for it on the other side. In his book, *Quality Wisdom For A Modern Age*, Denny delves into the Proverbs, unpacking the rich material contained therein, and has provided a concise and useful tool for us to apply these old Scriptural truths in todays "Modern Age." Whether you are looking for a quick reference guide or to dig deeper, I believe you have just found what you are looking for. Thank you, Denny, for sharing your love of the LORD with us, and for your desire to see others grow in His amazing Grace!
~ Leslie Rutten
Homemaker; Occupational Therapist

For anyone who desires to be obedient to the command "But prove yourselves doers of the word, and not merely hearers who delude themselves" (James 1:22 NASB) as it applies to the Book of Proverbs, then Denny's book will prove to be a well laid out tool. There are many useful resources included. The Subject Index alone makes the book worth having. It is a tremendous guide for topical searching.
Well done my friend,
~ Ron Bennett
Elder, Bible Teacher, Church at Sandhurst

Dr. Denny Bates has put together a simple, daily look at the promises of God that are declared in direction, woven to our souls in prayer. Men and women are transformed when they allow the living word of God to live in them. Each page of *Quality Wisdom For A Modern Age* is a promise of God, declared for today, brought to life in prayer. So that "Today May You" grow in the knowledge of the Greatness of God!
~ Dick Brown
Business Owner

In *Quality Wisdom For A Modern Age*, Dr. Denny Bates' commitment to make quality disciples for Jesus shines through in this collection of rich resources. If you desire to deepen your walk with Jesus and are looking for an easy to follow, systematic approach which also offers the flexibility of diving deeper, then look no more. Whether you desire a personal study or to make progress with others (QWMA) takes you on a journey through the wisdom of Proverbs, encouraging a closer walk with Jesus.
~ Lisa Ray
Retired Educator

James, the half-brother of Jesus, wrote under the inspiration of the Holy Spirit to the dispersed who were living in a world hostile to the gospel message … "But if any of you lacks wisdom, let him ask of God, who gives to all generously and without reproach, and it will be given to him" (James 1:5). Dr. H. Dennis Bates or Denny, my spiritual brother as well as my biological sibling, has written a resource just for those that would seek God's wisdom in a world that is still hostile to His message. *Quality Wisdom for a Modern Age* is an easy to use exploration of King Solomon's masterpiece on wisdom, Proverbs. It can be used as a devotional, a small group study or a guide for wisdom on different aspects of life as the need arises. I am truly looking forward to using it in my daily life in this complicated, complex world and am thankful that Solomon had it right when he wrote that there was nothing new under the sun; Only the names and the places change. The human experience is just that, the human experience and it never changes.
~ Tamara Bates-Rhodes, RN

You know it's going to be a good day when you encounter some quality wisdom first thing, walk with it and let it guide you throughout your day. And so, it is with the daily *Declarations of Quality Wisdom* from the Proverbs-based devotional book, *Quality Wisdom for a Modern Age,* by Denny Bates. This guidebook gives you one piece of wisdom each day for you to savor and incorporate into your daily practice. In turn providing a basis for personal growth which will spill over into your professional and spiritual life. It gives you the opportunity to apply that wisdom and live it loudly. Remember, what we say is heard in what we show. So, walk with the wisdom in this devotional and grow in greatness.
~ Dennis Arnst, PhD - Audiologist

Dr. Denny Bates has created an exegesis of Proverbs that is both rich and practical, with clear encouragement about how to live wisely in a modern community of Faith. The Lord's words are like goads; spurring us on, teaching, and admonishing. Aptly applied, God's Word is alive, critical and precious, changing the trajectory of our lives. Denny's book draws a thoughtful picture of how to best glean from the Proverbs, and how to strategically do what they say. Thank you Denny for allowing yourself to be a scholar, brother, and even more so a son. When you sent this for me to read, the Lord meant it as a balm and direction for my heart. This book is dynamic and concise, Spirit led, and a daily treasure of wisdom!
~ Dee Hoehn, M.A., L.P.C. Owner and Therapist Grace Counseling, LLC

Proverbs is well known as the book of wisdom. Having the opportunity of seeing Denny's heart and service for the Lord, I know his wisdom and insight will carry his readers on a deeper dive. Get ready for the journey.
~ Dexter Godfrey, Kingdom Power Couple

'In a society where the wisdom of the Bible is continually being pushed aside, it is refreshing to see a book published that makes The Proverbs applicable. Denny's heart to see this generation embrace the Truth and direction of the Proverbs is a light to follow through Quality Wisdom for a Modern Age"
~ Debra Lynn Hayes, author *RISE....What To Do When Hell Won't Back Off*

Most won't admit that they need it, but everyone needs guidance in today's modern age. Full of wisdom and a burning desire to always help others, Denny Bates does a great job of delivering this wisdom in a simple format.
~ John Chase, Financial Advisor

Dr. Bates uses the book of Proverbs to give simple yet profound words for each daily devotional with much attention to detail giving the reader points to ponder throughout his day. A good read.
~ Pam Clemons, retired RN

"Living in this world, we need all the wisdom we can get! The Proverbs are chock full of applicable tidbits and Dr. Bates does an amazing job at breaking it down into bite-size bits that we can digest on a daily basis. I thoroughly enjoy his approach and see it as something that anyone can implement daily--over and over!"
~ Renee Vidor, speaker, and community-creator, author of *Measuring Up: How to WIN in a World of Comparison*

In *Quality Wisdom for a Modern Age*, Dr. Denny Bates has, once again, provided a million-dollar tool for followers of Christ to develop discipleship habits and to live Kingdom lives. This resource could be used in a variety of ways and is full of "high-value wisdom" about life, about living for God, about dealing with people, and about living with situations. This work is a guaranteed GRAND SLAM for every disciple of Christ!!!
Dr. David Wike, Pastor Ebenezer Baptist Church

Quality Wisdom For A Modern Age embraces the teachings of Solomon as written in Proverbs. Timely lessons that respect our schedules yet provide an in-depth challenge encouraging us to assimilate and connect with coworkers, friends, and seekers we meet on life's road. Whether you use it as a study guide or a future reference book for all things Proverbs; check it out.
Tessy L. Baker, Ed.S School Psychologist

Quality Wisdom For A Modern Age is an insightful read that shows you how to recognize and apply the truth on a daily basis. Dr. Denny Bates provides an amazing resource that brings the wisdom and practical teaching from the book of Proverbs to life. Make it a part of your routine as you grow, lead, serve, and impact the world.
~ Jim Zugschwert, speaker, coach, and author of *Peak Perspective*

If there is a writer who can take the ancient words of the book of Proverbs and help us apply them to our present days, that writer is Dr. Denny Bates. Quality Wisdom for a Modern Age will challenge you and bless you in your professional and personal life as Dr. Bates guides you in hearing Proverbs with enlightened spirit-led ears. This book is a must-have!
~ Helen Rogers Dobbins BSN, RN Blogger for Sorrow into Dancing

Your very practical encouragement has always been a bright spot for me. Thank you for sharing this! I can't wait to see how God will continue to use you!
~ Abby Feistel, mom and blogger

Denny is a great friend and mentor of mine and has been for nearly two decades. In *Quality Wisdom for a Modern Age* you will find insight, perspective and truth that is deeply needed for life in this world. I cannot recommend this book more highly to you. It is a must use resource as you journey through life.
~ Reeves Cannon, M.A.,LPC, BCPCC, Executive Pastor, Church at Sandhurst

Quality Wisdom for a Modern Age is not book on leadership – it is a manual on how to incorporate proverbs into our daily lives to not only deal with the issues of daily life, but to anticipate them. Keep the book close to your nightstand, to use the analogy "Break glass in case of emergency", or to be inspired. Dr. Denny Bates uses daily declarations to assist individuals and leaders to help them in their daily duties. This is important as one must be able to lead themselves in order to lead others.
~ Len Clark, Ph.D. LTC Media

"Denny has a clear talent for packaging encouraging, Biblical content in a form that anyone can benefit from. *Quality Wisdom For A Modern Age* is another winner in his lineup of materials that can be used for a variety of settings and applications. I'm thankful for his contributions to the Body of Christ!"
~ Chris Honeycutt Lead Pastor, Forward /// Myrtle Beach

Dr Denny Bates is consistent in publishing *quality* resources that we can apply in our real lives. *Quality Wisdom for a Modern Age* is no different. Denny pours his mentorship onto paper again so we can turn to daily use in practical ways to become better, *quality* leaders.
~ Bo Myers: Husband, Father, Local ministry leader, Servant pastor, Deputy Coroner

About Dr. Denny Bates

Dr. Denny Bates is Principal Consultant for Quality Leadership Consultants, founder of Something New Christian Publishers, adjunct faculty mentor in the Columbia Biblical Seminary online Doctor of Ministerial Leadership program, and a founding member of the John Maxwell Team of certified coaches, speakers, and trainers. He has earned degrees from Francis Marion College [B.S.] and Columbia Biblical Seminary and School of Missions [MDiv, DMin]. With a doctoral degree in personal and organizational leadership, he is well equipped to serve as teacher, life coach, mentor, disciplemaker, motivational speaker and writer for his own leadership and personal growth titles as well as helping others write their stories*

Denny has written for an international publisher of Bible commentary, served as the Discipleship Pastor in the local church, as well as being a leader in the marketplace by creating the social networking brand #Aisle31. By God's grace, he seeks to live above the fray and "Press on!" Visit **www.dennybates.com**.

*See www.HelpMeWriteMyStory.com for this custom service.

www.ingramcontent.com/pod-product-compliance
Lightning Source LLC
LaVergne TN
LVHW061257060426
835508LV00015B/1401